the LEGO® ANIMATION book

MAKE YOUR OWN LEGO MOVIES!

DAVID PAGANO AND DAVID PICKETT

no starch press

Printed in Korea

Third Printing

20 19 18 17   3 4 5 6 7 8 9

ISBN-10: 1-59327-741-5
ISBN-13: 978-159327-741-3

Publisher: William Pollock
Production Editor: Riley Hoffman
Cover Design: Beth Middleworth
Developmental Editor: Tyler Ortman
Technical Reviewer: Chris Salt
Copyeditor: Rachel Monaghan
Compositor: Riley Hoffman
Proofreader: Lisa Devoto Farrell
Indexer: BIM Creatives, LLC

For information on distribution, translations, or bulk sales,
please contact No Starch Press, Inc. directly:

No Starch Press, Inc.
245 8th Street, San Francisco, CA 94103
phone: 1.415.863.9900; info@nostarch.com; www.nostarch.com

Library of Congress Cataloging-in-Publication Data

Names: Pagano, David, author. | Pickett, David (David M.), author.
Title: The LEGO animation book : make your own LEGO movies! / by David Pagano
   and David Pickett.
Description: San Francisco, CA : No Starch Press, Inc., [2016]
Identifiers: LCCN 2016013630 (print) | LCCN 2016016867 (ebook) | ISBN
   9781593277413 (pbk.) | ISBN 1593277415 (pbk.) | ISBN 9781593277895 (epub)
   | ISBN 159327789X (epub) | ISBN 9781593277901 (mobi) | ISBN 1593277903
   (mobi)
Subjects: LCSH: Stop-motion animation films. | Animation
   (Cinematography)--Instruments. | LEGO toys.
Classification: LCC TR897.6 .P34 2016 (print) | LCC TR897.6 (ebook) | DDC
   777/.7--dc23
LC record available at https://lccn.loc.gov/2016013630

Production Date: 12/6/17
Plant & Location: Printed by We SP Corp, Seoul, South Korea
Job / Batch #: 80671 / We SP 112017 R1

To Steph, a fiercely loyal friend. You'd be delighted to know I'm still at it.

—David

To Bert, for his love, patience, and support.

—Dave

Contents

Introduction

You're about to dive deep into the heart of LEGO animation and filmmaking! It only gets stranger—and more fun—from here.

Our goal was to create a definitive reference for folks of all ages and skill levels, from the 8-year-old YouTuber to the 45-year-old AFOL (adult fan of LEGO) and beyond. We've structured things so that you don't need to read the book from cover to cover all at once—though we'd love it if you did.

If you're brand-new to LEGO animation, start with Chapter 1, which introduces some key concepts to get your feet wet. If you're already knee deep in the LEGO animation hobby, you might be looking to sharpen a specific skill. That's cool. Feel free to skip around, skim, or read upside down. You won't hurt our feelings.

If at any point you feel compelled to stop reading and start animating, please do so. No amount of prose can take the place of practice. We'll be here waiting when you need us again.

But wait—who exactly are "we"? Allow us to introduce ourselves . . .

You can use *The LEGO Animation Book* any way you want, but we don't recommend eating it.

DAVID PAGANO

Born: 1985
Middle name: Michael
Wears glasses: Yes
Has facial hair: Often

First LEGO animation: 1995
Prefers brick-built special effects to CGI: Always
Place in the 2008 Nicktoons "Built by Me"
　LEGO animation contest: 2nd (tie)

Hi there! I'm David Pagano, one half of *The LEGO Animation Book* duo. I run a studio called Paganomation, where my team and I create stop-motion shorts, ads, and music videos. Since 2007, we've made dozens of LEGO animations that have appeared on LEGO.com, YouTube, Disney XD, and Nickelodeon and for approximately two seconds in the climax of *The LEGO Movie*. You might also be familiar with some of my original films, like *Little Guys!* or *Playback* (where I introduced the large-scale characters seen in Chapter 5).

DAVID PICKETT

Born: 1985
Middle name: Michael
Wears glasses: Yes
Has facial hair: Rarely

First LEGO animation: 1998
Prefers brick-built special effects to CGI: Always
Place in the 2008 Nicktoons "Built by Me"
　LEGO animation contest: 2nd (tie)

Hello! I'm David Pickett, and I'm excited to teach you about animation! I'm a self-taught animator with no formal training, but that hasn't stopped me from making award-winning LEGO animations like *Nightly News at Nine*, *Metamorphosis*, and *Choose Your Own Storyline: The Fight for Paradise Hills*. I'm best known for my YouTube channel BRICK 101, where I share my animations, custom creations, and LEGO set reviews.

Meet the stars of *The Magic Picnic*: Anna, Matt, and Shaun (the picnic basket).

About the Companion Film

There's another important duo you need to meet: Anna and Matt. They're here to illustrate LEGO animation techniques. But they're more than just pretty faces—they're also the main characters of a short film we've produced as a companion to this book, *The Magic Picnic*.

Nearly every shot in *The Magic Picnic* showcases an important LEGO animation concept or idea (though some are there simply because we thought they looked cool). You might want to watch the film before reading the book, just to enjoy the story and to see what's possible with LEGO animation. Later, you can come back to the movie with newfound knowledge and see how the approaches we discuss in the book look onscreen.

You can find *The Magic Picnic* on the book's website (*https://www.nostarch.com/legoanimation/*).

A Word About LEGO Animation

When we talk about *LEGO animation* or *brickfilms*, we're talking about something specific: stop-motion animated films created with LEGO bricks and elements.

Stop-motion is an animation technique almost as old as motion pictures themselves. It involves taking many still photographs of an object. An animator moves the object a tiny amount after each photo is taken. Then, the pictures are viewed in sequence (like a flipbook) and the illusion of movement is achieved.

LEGO animation is a *medium* (like live-action film, photography, painting, or writing), not a *genre* (like comedy, drama, action, or romance). You'll come across all kinds of brickfilms—stories, music videos, advertisements, tutorials, and more. That said, there are a couple of things we *aren't* talking about when we say "LEGO animation": computer-generated animations of LEGO bricks and characters, and live-action footage of LEGO models being manipulated by a human.

We use the terms *animator* and *brickfilmer* to refer to anyone who creates LEGO animation. Today's LEGO filmmakers are kids, adults, girls, boys, parents, teachers, students, and everything in between. You may not consider yourself an animator or filmmaker yet, but our goal is to change that. Let's get to it!

A stop-motion photo sequence. Notice that tiny movements have been made between each image.

Anyone can be a LEGO animator!

1 The Basics

The world of LEGO animation: where inanimate plastic objects come to life. If this is your first foray into brickfilming, welcome! This chapter will teach you the basic skills you need to make your first animation. Later chapters will build on this base to help you become an expert animator.

What You'll Need

With digital cameras becoming cheaper and more sophisticated every year, the hardware to create brickfilms is easy to acquire. There's no need to spend money on fancy equipment; you probably have everything you need to get started sitting around your house right now.

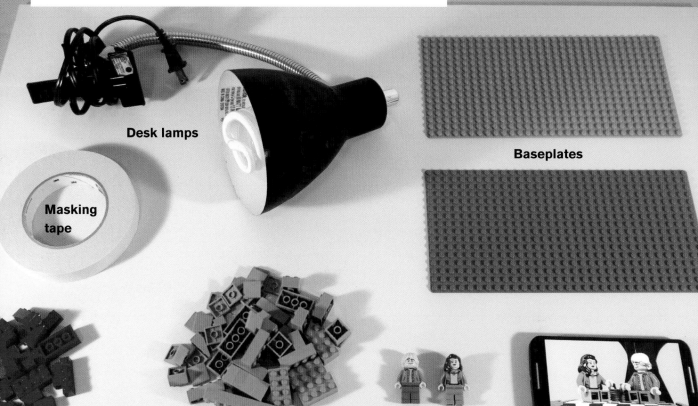

Desk lamps

Masking tape

Baseplates

Assorted bricks

Minifigures

Camera

Posterboard

You can use any camera for LEGO animation, but a smartphone is the easiest for beginners.

Step 1: **Grab a Camera**

The camera is your primary tool for capturing the worlds you create. For your first animation, we recommend using a smartphone or tablet running the Stop Motion Studio app by Cateater (available for iOS, Android, Kindle, and Windows devices). By keeping the technical setup simple, you can focus on the fun part: animating.

If you don't have a smartphone, use a camera you're comfortable with. This could be a simple point-and-shoot camera, a high-end DSLR, or even a webcam. If it takes pictures, you can animate with it. See Chapter 6 for a more detailed rundown of camera options.

If you're using a brand-new camera that you aren't familiar with yet, read the instruction manual or watch online tutorials to get up to speed on the basic functions. If you're feeling really ambitious, consider taking a photography class or two.

Step 2: **Set Up Your Studio**

Now it's time to set up your animation studio. Find a flat, stable surface that you're comfortable working at. A table or desk is ideal. This will be your *animation surface*.

Place the animation surface somewhere that's out of the way—preferably in a room where there aren't a lot of windows and with a door that you can close.

Stop-motion is a delicate craft, and we don't recommend animating in areas with heavy foot traffic. Make sure there are electrical sockets nearby so you can plug in your lights, camera, computer, and so on.

Once you're set up, get comfortable . . . you'll be in this spot for long periods of time.

You should be able to take decent pictures using any overhead light fixtures in your room. If you have a couple of desk lamps, you can use those, too. The goal is to have as much control over your lighting as possible.

Set up your camera at about the same height as your animation surface. You can accomplish this using a tripod or a camera cradle (see Chapter 6 for more details). If you don't have either of these things, you can build your own camera cradle out of—what else?—LEGO bricks.

Be careful with lights; they can get hot. Ask an adult for help. (If you are an adult, ask yourself for help.)

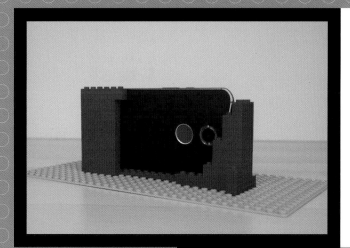

Don't make your camera cradle more complicated than it needs to be.

Build a Camera Cradle

1. Grab a baseplate and some bricks (don't worry about color).
2. Set your camera on the baseplate.
3. Build a structure around the camera to hold it in place. Make sure not to block the buttons or the camera lens.
4. When your camera cradle is complete, secure the baseplate to your animation surface using clamps or masking tape.

More characters mean more work. Start small and work your way up.

Build a Scene

Now comes the fun part: building your first scene! Imagination is one of an animator's greatest assets, and you might have all sorts of crazy ideas for things you want to animate. If this is your first animation, we recommend keeping it simple. The more activity there is in a scene, the longer it will take to animate. Instead of jumping right into an epic battle between dozens of robots and cheerleaders, start with just one robot and one cheerleader performing some basic actions.

The backdrop for your first animation shouldn't be overly complicated, either. It can be as simple as a baseplate in front of a piece of posterboard or an official LEGO model.

Once your scene is set up, secure anything you don't want to move (the camera cradle, the set, etc.) with clamps, masking tape, or sticky tack. Now you're ready to animate!

We used a 20"×30" sheet of sky-blue posterboard for the sky in *The Magic Picnic*.

READY TO ANIMATE? SURE— ALTHOUGH I PREFER WRITING OUT A SCRIPT, CREATING SKETCHES AND STORYBOARDS, AND PLANNING MY FILMS IN DETAIL.

PLANNING IS NICE, BUT SOMETIMES YOU JUST NEED TO JUMP IN. FOR MOST OF MY EARLY ANIMATIONS, I MADE UP THE STORY AS I WENT ALONG AND FILMED WITHOUT USING ANY SOFTWARE. I THINK IT'S MORE IMPORTANT TO HAVE FUN AND START ANIMATING THAN TO BE TOTALLY PREPARED.

Step 3: Animate

This is what you've been waiting for—animation. Arrange your characters (or whatever you're animating) in front of the camera and take a picture; this is also called *capturing a frame*. Next, move your characters slightly. Then, take another picture. Repeat these steps until you've done all the movements you want to do.

Tips for Your First Animation

- Before you start animating, think about what you want your characters to do. Where will they start, and where will they end up? How will they get there?
- Don't worry about how tiny the movements should be between pictures. For now, just do what feels right. You can adjust things later to improve the final product.
- Be careful not to accidentally bump your animation surface, camera, or set. These *set bumps* can produce unexpected results.

If it feels like you're not getting the hang of animation as quickly as you'd like, fear not. In Chapter 2, we'll take a close look at how to animate LEGO minifigures. And in Chapter 3, we'll cover some fundamental principles for animating just about anything.

To take a picture in Stop Motion Studio, just press the big red button. Don't worry—nothing will self-destruct.

Basic Cinematography

Here are a few tips for taking great photos!

Compose a shot. (Keep the subject in frame, and keep your fingers out!)

Adjust the focus. (This helps you avoid "everything is blurry" syndrome.)

Set the exposure. (Let there be light!)

Does your photo look like any of these goofy photos? If it does, you might want to spend some more time learning how to operate your camera (check out Chapter 8 for more tips).

Watching your animation in Stop Motion Studio is as simple as pressing the white triangle.

Step 4: Watch Your Animation

It's time to sit back and enjoy the fruits of your labor. Now that you're done taking pictures, you'll need to turn them into a video.

If you used Stop Motion Studio or a similar app, you can simply press a button to watch your animation. This is a great way to check your progress as you're animating and make sure the characters are moving the way you intended. Once you're happy with the final product, you can export a video file or upload directly to a video-hosting service like YouTube.

If you used a camera without stop-motion software, you'll need to transfer the images to a computer and use video-editing software to compile those images. For more on editing, jump ahead to Chapter 9.

Step 5: Adjust the Frame Rate

When you watched your animation, did the characters move at the right speed? You can make your characters move faster or slower by adjusting the *frame rate*. The frame rate refers to how many pictures appear in every second of your video, and it is measured in *frames per second (FPS)*. Most brickfilmers animate at 12 or 15 FPS. American TV shows and movies are usually 24 or 30 FPS.

The higher the FPS, the smoother the motion will look. But a higher frame rate also means you'll need to take more pictures for the same amount of animation. In other words, if you were animating a 1-minute film at 10 FPS, you'd have to take 600 pictures, but if you animated the same film at 30 FPS, you'd have to take 1,800 pictures!

5 FPS = fewer pictures + bigger movements.

10 FPS = more pictures + smaller movements.

15 FPS = even more pictures + teeny-tiny movements.

Use the gear icon to adjust your FPS in Stop Motion Studio.

Play your animation at a few different frame rates to see which you like best. Expert animators usually pick a frame rate before they start animating (more on this in Chapter 8), but we find it's easier for beginners to do this step last.

Next Steps

So you've made your first animation, and now you have follow-up questions: Why is there so much flickering light? How do I add sound? Can I make my characters fly? Is stopping to sleep and eat *really* all that important?

Throughout the rest of this book, we'll answer these questions and guide you toward creating an epic animation masterpiece. But before moving on to Chapter 2, take a moment to reflect on the animation you just made:

- What was the most successful part of your animation, and why?
- What problems did you encounter while animating? How did you overcome them?

- What would you like to do in your next animation that you didn't do in this one?
- If you showed your animation to an audience, did they respond how you wanted them to?
- What did you learn from this animation?

No matter how old or how experienced you are, it's important to keep learning, asking questions, and reflecting on your own progress. Every new animation project is an opportunity to improve your skills, and even mistakes can become successes if they help you make something better the next time around.

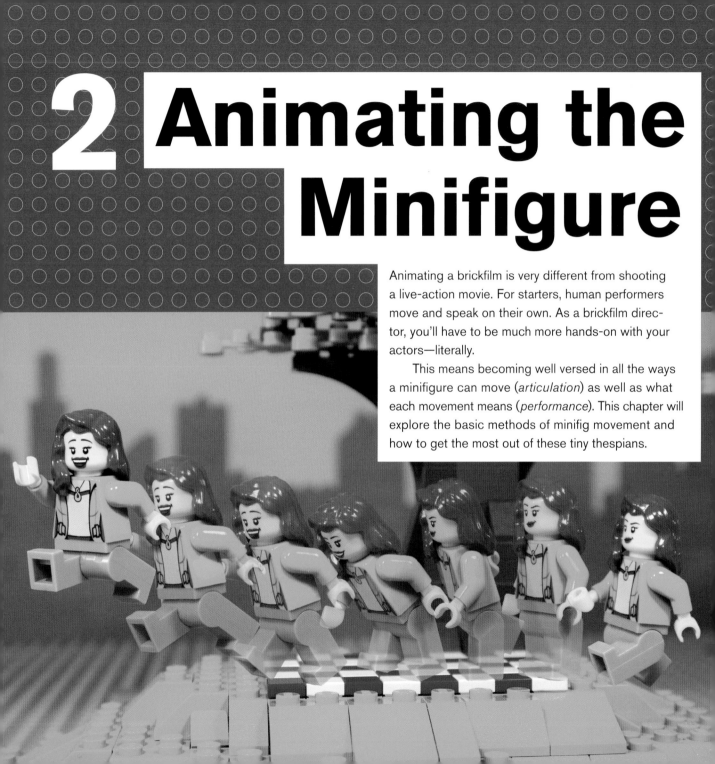

2 Animating the Minifigure

Animating a brickfilm is very different from shooting a live-action movie. For starters, human performers move and speak on their own. As a brickfilm director, you'll have to be much more hands-on with your actors—literally.

This means becoming well versed in all the ways a minifigure can move (*articulation*) as well as what each movement means (*performance*). This chapter will explore the basic methods of minifig movement and how to get the most out of these tiny thespians.

Know Your Minifigure

The first thing to understand about minifigures is how each body part moves. Even though you control your minifig's behavior, their bodies do have physical limits.

The most obvious limit? Minifigures don't have knees. If you want a character to kneel like a human being, you may be frustrated to find that your actor can't deliver. We recommend highlighting what minifigs *can* do rather than expecting the impossible.

Full-Body Poses

Minifigs have seven primary *points of articulation*. These are the places where you can twist or rotate a body part: the neck, the shoulders, the wrists, and the hips. The best way to learn your way around a minifig is through practice—go grab one now so you can test out each joint as we explain it.

Neck

Minifigs can rotate their heads all the way around, a full 360 degrees. The neck also allows the head to move up and down a little bit without disconnecting. Unfortunately, minifigs can't tilt their heads forward and backward (to nod) or from side to side. Some larger minifigure hair pieces (like Anna's) make it difficult to rotate the head without taking the hair off first.

Shoulders

The shoulders allow the arms to rotate in a full circle. However, if your actor is wearing head-gear, is sporting shoulder accessories, or just has big hair like Anna, they may not be able to rotate their arms all the way around.

Because of how their arms move, minifigs are really good at picking up and pointing at items directly in front of them, but they are totally awkward when it comes to doing jumping jacks or grabbing anything directly to their left or right. Keep this in mind when positioning props on your set.

With minifigures, the phrase "watch your back" takes on a whole new meaning.

Matt can "raise the roof," but Anna's hair gets in the way.

Hips

Minifig hips allow the legs to extend straight out in front and bend back slightly. Minifigs are really good at walking, kicking, sitting, and bending forward but not so good at doing yoga or splits.

Wrists

Minifigure hands can rotate 360 degrees. When you're filming a scene, it can be hard to use your gigantic human hands to rotate your actors' wrists without knocking everything over. We recommend using a toothpick for positioning hands.

You can also pop minifig hands out of their sockets. This is a great way to add a little extra distance when your actor is reaching for the sky.

Hip rotations can make a big difference in a minifigure's pose. Anna leans back and prepares to take action, while Matt sits down to relax.

Keep a toothpick handy for really subtle wrist movements and adjustments.

Matt got so excited in this scene that his hands popped out of their sockets.

Minuscule Movements

In addition to the seven primary points of articulation, there are six secondary points of articulation: the scalp, the waist, the hands, and the feet. These don't allow for the same amount of movement as the primary points, but they still contribute to the overall posing of your minifigs.

Scalp

The *scalp* refers to the stud on top of a minifigure's head. This is where hair and other headgear attach to the head. Headgear that doesn't go below the shoulders (like Matt's hair) can rotate freely around the head. Anything that does go below the shoulders (like Anna's hair) has a restricted range of movement. You can disconnect headgear to move it up and down. This is useful for when a minifig is surprised, scratching their head, or putting on a helmet.

Waist

The waist is where the legs attach to the torso. On a typical minifig, the only motion possible here is to pull apart the legs and torso a bit to stretch your minifig a little higher. However, if your minifig has brick-built legs, you can use an old-style torso and an offset plate to enable your character to twist at the waist. (Note: this will slightly damage the torso.)

Matt reaches for the sky while Anna uses a retro torso to turn sideways.

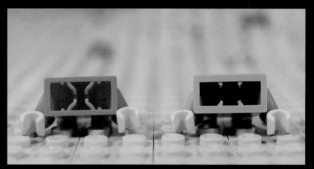

Modern-style torsos like Matt's (left) can't sit on an offset plate. Torsos produced before 1999 can, though it does slightly damage the torso (right).

I'M NOT A HUGE FAN OF ALTERING LEGO PIECES, BUT I'LL DO IT IF IT'S SUBTLE AND MAKES THE ANIMATION PROCESS GO FASTER.

I NEVER HESITATE TO STRESS, MODIFY, CUT, OR GLUE MY LEGO PIECES IF IT WILL HELP ME REALIZE MY ARTISTIC VISION. *FOR ART!*

Hands

Minifig hands are more versatile than you might think. They can grasp a wide range of elements in the LEGO system, like plates, tiles, and cylindrical "bar" elements. Once in hand, these elements can slide up and down and wiggle back and forth. Flipping the hand around so the rounded side is on top can change the angle at which a minifigure holds an object or prop. The flat side of the hand can also be built upon like a stud.

Feet

When a minifig is on a baseplate, each foot grips onto a stud. You can tilt a minifig from side to side, which is great for depicting impatient characters. You can also twist the minifig side to side a little bit, helping to make up for the fact that minifigs can't twist at the waist.

With only one foot connected to the ground, a minifig has an even greater range of motion. A one-foot stud connection is perfect for twirling ballet dancers. If your minifig is sitting down, the holes in the back of the legs let them rock back and forth.

Even minifigs like to build with LEGO elements!

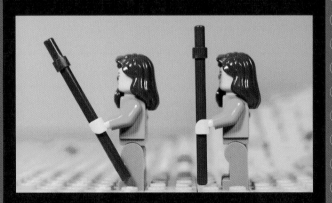

The angle of the arm is the same on both Annas. The only difference is that her hand is flipped.

Twisting is easier on smooth surfaces, like tiles. Tilting is easier on studded surfaces.

Minifigs can twirl on one stud or rock back and forth while sitting.

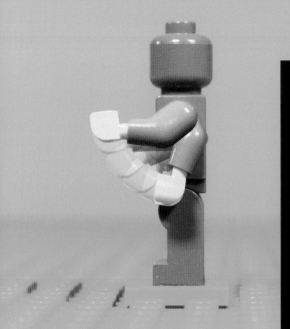

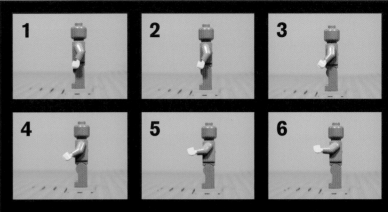

For the arm lift, we're showing you the individual frames. For the rest of the gestures, we'll just show key poses and let you use your imagination to fill in the rest.

Body Language

Now that you've seen the different ways you can move your minifigs, it's time to give those movements some meaning. Every action should say something about what your character is thinking or feeling and should contribute to the story you're telling.

Basic Gestures

Gestures are any movements that help reinforce a character's dialogue or emotional state. They allow minifigures to communicate even when their mouths aren't moving. The following gestures are the basic components of minifig body language.

Arm Lifts and Drops

Arm lifts and arm drops are the bread and butter of minifig gestures. Lifting one arm generally shows that a character has an idea they want to share: "I'm going to eat that waffle." Dropping an arm indicates dissent: "No, I will not eat that waffle!" A well-timed arm lift can emphasize a word in a sentence: "I'm *going* to eat that waffle" versus "I'm going to eat *that* waffle."

Lifting both arms quickly implies excitement or surprise: "Waffles!? I love waffles!" Conversely, a slow double-arm drop can serve as a sigh of defeat: "Oh well, I guess I'll eat these waffles, even though there's no syrup."

Hand Twist

The hand twist is a subtle gesture you can use to indicate possibilities or uncertainty. An inward twist can be used as an invitation: "Help me build my doomsday machine." An outward twist can indicate that there is another option to consider: "Or face my wrath." Twisting back and forth means the character is not entirely sure about something: "The doomsday machine should be operational in *a week or two*."

Double-Hand Twist

Twisting both hands outward simultaneously is a sort of shrug or turning out of pockets. It can indicate a lack of ideas. Twisting both hands inward might show that a character is resolving an argument or explaining a plan. Quickly twisting hands inward and outward is the minifigure equivalent of "jazz hands." It can be used to express delight, excitement, or a feeling of being overwhelmed.

Head Shake

Minifigures can shake their heads like pros. A fast head shake generally means "No! No way. No siree." A slow head shake with pauses on each turn can show that your character is confused or thinking about something. A minifig shaking their head slowly while bent forward and covering their face could be expressing shame, regret, or sadness.

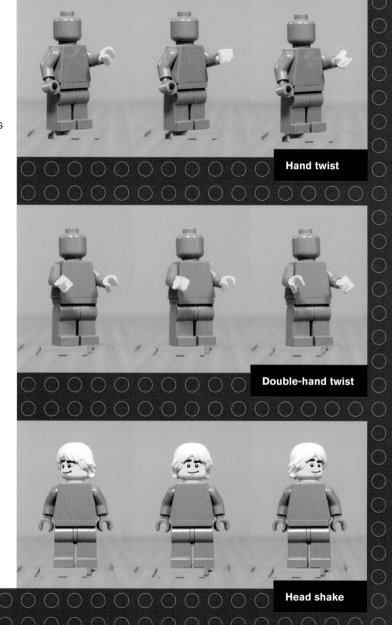

Hand twist

Double-hand twist

Head shake

Head Pop

A head pop can convey that a character is surprised. It can be accompanied by the headgear popping off the head for added dramatic effect.

Bend at the Waist

Bending at the waist can indicate a lot about a minifig's state of mind. If they bend back, they might be surprised, taken aback, deep in thought, relaxing, or just trying to look up. If they bend forward, they might be sad, resigned, grateful, or showing respect. If they rock back and forth, they might be nervous. Also, since minifigures can't nod, they sometimes make a quick bow to show their agreement.

Pivot

Minifigures can't twist at the waist, but they can pivot on their feet. A quick pivot might be a reaction to something surprising, while a slow pivot might be an attempt to get a closer look at something. In addition to pivoting, minifigs can lean side to side on their feet. This is great for when a character needs to be sneaky and peek around a corner or tilt side to side impatiently.

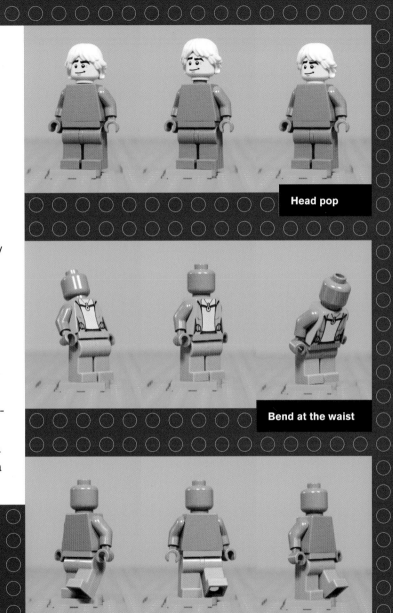

Head pop

Bend at the waist

Pivot

Complex Gestures

Once you've got a handle on the basics, you can combine gestures for more intricate expressions. The following list features some complex gestures your minifigures can perform—but don't hesitate to create combinations of your own, too! Mix and match the basics, and see what else you can come up with.

Arm Nod

Minifigs can't nod their heads, but they can show agreement in other ways. The arm nod is a versatile workaround. Simply have your minifig quickly lift and drop an arm while bending forward and back to show they agree with another character. To help get the timing right, try acting out a short nod of agreement yourself. How far did you tilt your head on the way up? Did you move your head faster on the way down? If a character does an arm nod while no one else is around, it can show that they just had an idea—a "eureka!" moment.

Lift, Drop, and Twist

A single-arm lift coupled with some inward and outward hand twists is a great way to wave hello. A slow double-arm lift combined with an outward double-hand twist can convey a realistic shrug. If things get really crazy, your minifig might flail their arms up and down while twisting their hands around.

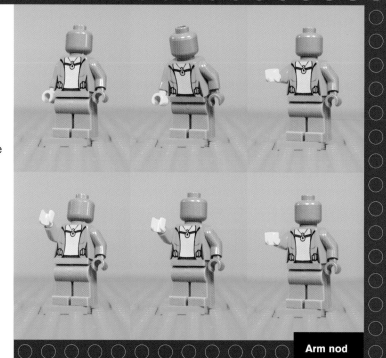

Arm nod

Head Scratch

The head scratch is a perfect way to communicate that a minifig doesn't have a clue what's going on. They lift their arm up to their hair. They twist their hand back and forth, and their hair piece moves slightly from side to side.

Point and Pivot

For dramatic scenes, a minifig might pivot on their foot while lifting their arm to point at something important: "My cat's stuck in that tree!"

Double Take

The double take is a great comedic gesture for showing surprise. A minifig briefly looks at something, turns away for a moment, and then suddenly looks back—but on the second look, their head and hair pop up a bit: "What was that?!"

Dejected Foot Kick

A dejected foot kick shows that a character is feeling sad or discouraged. The minifig halfheartedly kicks one foot forward a little bit while bending forward: "Better luck next time, Charlie Brown . . ."

Full-Body Freak-Out

If a minifig is surprised, disgusted, or excited beyond all belief, they might spasm wildly—flailing their arms and hands while leaning back and kicking up a leg all at the same time: "Waffles?! I have to have some *NOW*!"

Exercise: Show Your Feelings

Now that you've learned about gestures, it's time to put them to use! For this exercise, you'll make a very short animation (2 to 5 seconds) of a minifigure expressing an emotion using only their body language.

Place a minifig in front of your camera and choose an emotion: happy, sad, angry, surprised, afraid, disgusted, excited, guilty, ashamed, bored, proud, energetic, confused, anxious, content, or anything else you can imagine. What do *you* do when you feel this emotion? Can you translate that action to the minifig?

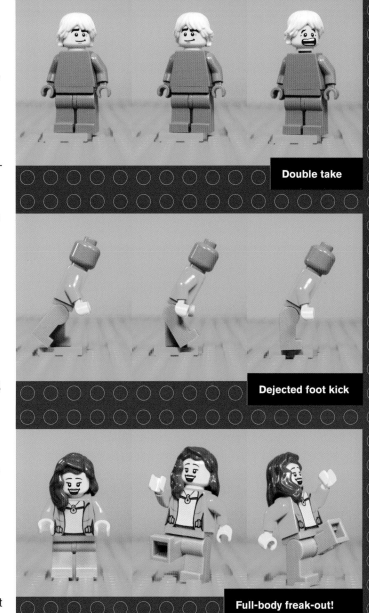

Double take

Dejected foot kick

Full-body freak-out!

Walking

Walking is an action that many people take for granted. However, walking actually takes a great deal of coordination—just ask any toddler. In this section, we'll go over how to animate your minifig's walk and how you can use different walks to express a certain mood or emotion.

A Solid Foundation

One of the tricky parts of animating a character walking is that they will frequently be off-balance and easy to knock over. In traditional stop-motion animation, characters' feet are often attached to the set so that they don't fall over. These attachment points are called *tie-downs*. Fortunately, minifigs have built-in tie-downs, since their feet can attach firmly to baseplates. (Thank goodness for clutch power.)

If you need your character to walk on a smooth surface, you can use putty as a tie-down. Just be aware that it could leave residue that you'll have to clean up between frames. You can also keep your surface *mostly* tiled but have a 1×1 plate hidden underneath your character's foot. That was our solution for attaching Anna and Matt to their picnic blanket in *The Magic Picnic*.

Animating a walk on LEGO tiles is tough (even for us veterans), so we recommend doing your first walking animation on a studded surface.

Use putty as a tie-down on tiled surfaces.

Anna, Matt, and the picnic basket were attached to the picnic blanket using hidden 1×1 plates.

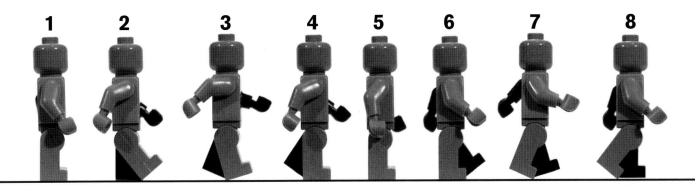

1 2 3 4 5 6 7 8

The standard minifigure walk cycle. Note that positions 3 and 7 have the figure's legs balanced between studs.

The Basic Walk Cycle

People-watching is an essential skill for every animator. Next time you're out in a public place, watch how people walk: their arms and legs move in a synchronized pattern. This sequence is known as a *walk cycle*.

Let's start by focusing on the legs. In the standard walk cycle, the minifigure legs take these steps:

1. The minifigure is standing still.
2. They move one foot forward (in this example, the right foot).
3. As the right foot moves forward, their weight shifts forward, and the left foot starts to lift off the ground.
4. As the right foot touches down, the left foot lifts farther off the ground.
5. The right foot is stationary as the left foot swings past it.
6. The left foot moves forward while the right foot stays still.
7. As the left foot starts to touch down, the right foot starts to lift.
8. The left foot plants on the ground as the right foot lifts off.

And then the cycle repeats, starting back at step 1.

Now, notice how the arms move. They help keep the body balanced by moving opposite of the legs. When the left leg is moving forward, the left arm is moving back, and vice versa.

The best way to become familiar with a minifigure walk cycle is to try it out. Follow the diagram above to animate your first walk test.

You can also download this diagram from the book's website (*https://www.nostarch.com/legoanimation/*).

Tips on Animating a Minifigure Walk Cycle

- Steps 3 and 7 are the hardest, because they require balancing the minifigure between studs. If your character feels loose or keeps falling over, you can use putty to hold them in place.
- Try to keep your character's torso upright. It will tend to tilt back and forth as you adjust the legs, which can lead to some wobbly walks.
- If your animation software has an onion-skinning feature (more on this in Chapter 6), this is a great time to use it. It will help you keep track of which step you're on.

- If you need to keep track of where your character's walk begins and ends, you can use color-coded LEGO pieces. Place them as markers on the edges of your set (outside of the camera's view).

These walk and run cycles work really well for animations displayed at 12 to 15 FPS. If you are animating at 5 or 10 FPS, you may want to cut steps 3 and 7 out of the walk cycle or your character will look like they're walking slowly. If you're animating at 20 FPS or higher, you'll probably need to add more steps in between these. (You might also want to reconsider your decision to film at such a high frame rate.)

If your minifigure successfully made it from point A to point B, congratulations! Completing a walk cycle is a huge milestone for every animator.

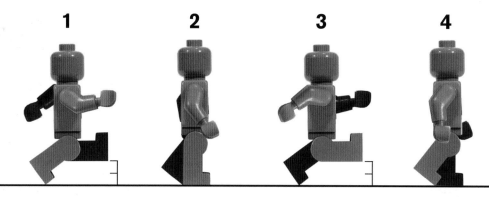

A minifigure run cycle. Note that the front foot in poses 1 and 3 lifts to a height of two plates above the ground. You can use transparent plates to support minifigs in these poses.

Unusual Walks

Walking can also be an opportunity to express something about a character. *How* do they move? Do they stagger, stumble, or skip? Do they prance, parade, or prowl? You can build on a basic walk to create something more expressive and complex. There are an infinite number of weird and silly walks to try, and each one can reveal something about your character's feelings or environment.

Not every "walk" needs to be graceful. In this example from *The Magic Picnic*, Matt stumbles backward on an alien planet.

A STANDARD WALK IS ONE OF THE RARE BITS OF ANIMATION THAT HAS A CLEAR-CUT FORMULA; YOU CAN PRACTICE IT OVER AND OVER AGAIN UNTIL YOU MASTER IT. THEN, YOU CAN BUILD ON THE BASIC WALK BY ADDING GESTURES.

I DON'T LIKE ANIMATING WALK CYCLES, SO I TRY TO AVOID THEM. THAT'S WHY I MAKE ANIMATIONS ABOUT A NEWS TEAM. MY CHARACTERS SIT AT DESKS OR STAND AT THE SCENE OF A NEWS STORY. THEY GESTURE A LOT, BUT THEY RARELY WALK.

Facial Animation

Human actors can easily convey a lot of information with subtle facial expressions, but minifigs are more limited.

Some brickfilmers choose to avoid facial animation entirely and give their characters the same expression throughout the whole film, which is a perfectly valid artistic choice (and great for beginners). For those who really want to pursue facial animation, there are three options: purist replacement, custom replacement, and digital animation.

Purist Replacement Techniques

With purist replacement facial animation, you use only official LEGO heads for your characters and swap them in and out between frames to change your characters' facial expressions.

Be sure to put the new head in the same position as the previous head so that the facial expression is the only thing that changes. If the change from one face to another looks too jarring, try hiding it in the middle of a head shake.

Replacement animation: instead of moving the same object in between frames, you remove one object (like Anna's head) and replace it with another.

Take a look through your collection of minifigure heads and see if you can find a few heads with different expressions that look similar enough to be the same character. Pay attention to features like lips, eyebrow color, and facial hair. When we designed Anna and Matt, we spent quite a while picking out a set of heads for each of them.

Purist replacement animation is great at conveying emotions and attitudes, but it's tough for making characters' mouths look like they're talking. If you want to sync a minifig's lips to their dialogue, you'll need to use one of the next two techniques.

We recommend sorting your minifig heads by color and facial features so that you can easily find multiple faces for a single character.

The many faces of Anna and Matt

Custom Replacement Techniques

If you're committed to minifigure lip syncing but don't want to spend hours and hours on digital animation, you can make or buy custom minifig heads. *Minifigs.me* sells a set of 12 heads that cover the basic phonetic mouth shapes. If you want to go the DIY route, you can attach facial features to a head using stickers or putty, or you can paint a set of faces onto some blank heads.

Whether you make or buy your custom heads, lip syncing is an advanced technique that requires a lot of prep work. We'll talk through that prep work in Chapter 9.

Digital Facial Animation

The most common type of digital facial animation is adding mouth shapes to make minifigs look like they're talking. But you can also give them all sorts of expressions. This is a very time-consuming process—which we'll cover in Chapter 9—but the end results look fantastic.

Matt tries on a *Minifigs.me* head while his cousin Mort shows off some homemade expressions.

You can use digital facial animation to have characters wink, frown, gasp, or make any other facial expression you can imagine.

Jumping, Flying, and Floating

Now your actors can walk and talk. But what if you want to make them jump or fly? Gravity can be a nuisance for stop-motion animators, but there are several creative ways to work around it.

In-Camera Techniques

Whenever possible, we recommend animating moves like jumping or flying on-set, rather than trying to do it digitally later. The main solution is to use hidden *support rigs*. If your minifig is only going to be in the air for a couple of frames, you can use a few small, transparent pieces to hold them in place. Your audience probably won't even notice.

Another great way to hide support rigs is to take advantage of what your camera can't see. You could hold the character up with a support that's hidden just outside of the frame or behind the character. If all else fails, you can hang something from a piece of clear thread.

Matt appears to float in midair . . .

. . . thanks to a hidden support rig and a little bit of putty. Take that, gravity!

Step 1: Take a picture with the object held in the air by the rig.

Step 2: Remove the object and the rig and take a picture of the background.

Advanced Levitation

For advanced animators, the best way to make things fly, float, or otherwise levitate is to build a support rig and then mask it out during post-production. Your rig can be as simple as a LEGO piece and some putty to hold the object in place. Then you take two pictures: one of the scene with the object and rig in place and one with them removed.

In post-production (which we'll cover in Chapter 9), you'll layer the image with the rig over the background image in photo-editing software (we recommend GIMP or Adobe Photoshop). Use an eraser tool to erase the rig so that the background from the second image shows through. Masking adds a lot of time to post-production, but the final product looks fantastic.

Step 3: Layer the two images in your photo editor and erase the rig.

Thinking Outside the Joints

Some brickfilm actors take the expression "break a leg" quite literally. If you're frustrated by the limitations of minifig joints, then you might want to consider modifying your minifigures to expand their acting repertoire.

Want a minifig to reach out to the side? Pop the arm off and stick it to the side of the torso with putty. Using this technique, you can make your minifig move their arm in new exciting ways: they can cover their mouth to cough or yawn, they can rub their belly, and they can even clap their hands. You'll need to make sure the putty sticks well enough to hold the arm up, and camouflage the putty so your audience doesn't notice it.

By switching a right arm with a left arm (or vice versa), you can make it look like a character bent their elbow backward. This may look a little unnatural as a still image, but using it in a frame or two can emphasize a throw or flail.

You can also rearrange a minifig's legs. It turns out that minifigures actually can kneel—sort of—if you flip their legs around at the waist and pop one leg out of the hips. You can also swap a left leg for a right leg mid-kick to make it look like the foot is bending at the ankle.

If you look closely, you can see the yellow putty holding the purple arm in place.

By rearranging some arms and legs, Anna and Matt can pose in fun new ways.

Brick-Built Limbs

Another way to circumvent the limited joints of minifigs is to build limbs to replace their normal ones.

The easiest thing to replace on a minifig is the legs. Some minifigs wear a slope-brick "dress"—and that's just the beginning of what you can do. If your character is a robot, you can give them any number of weird science-fiction-y legs. If your character is a gymnast, you can build special legs that allow them to do a split.

Arms are harder to replace than legs, so you'll have to use some creative techniques to make this work. Depending on the type of minifigure torso you're working with (pre-1999 or post-1999), you can replace the arms with control sticks or with bar-width accessories.

Old torsos like the one on the right can fit bar-width elements in the arm sockets. Modern torsos like the one on the left can hold control sticks in the arm sockets.

Mattborg and Cyberanna use advanced techniques to replace regular minifig arms and legs with more versatile brick-built limbs.

BRICK-BUILT LIMBS SHOULD MATCH YOUR CHARACTER'S DESIGN. OTHERWISE, YOUR AUDIENCE MIGHT INTERPRET "PERSON WITH A ROBOT ARM" AS "PERSON WITH NO ARM WHO HAS SOME WEIRD THING FLOATING NEXT TO THEM."

If you're feeling really adventurous, you can replace minifig parts with other pieces. If you want a character with a moving mouth, why not replace the head with a LEGO shark or alligator?

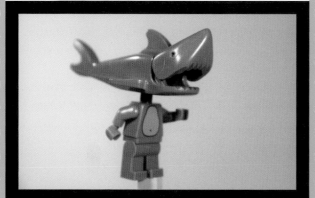

If your character needs to bite something or sing an opera, consider giving them a shark head.

Animating Characters with Limited Articulation

Certain specialized figures are far less posable than the average minifig. Some come with legs that can't bend, others can't twist their hands, and still others are just one solid piece. Animating these characters requires extra creativity. If your character has short legs, they might wobble rather than walk. If your character doesn't have any points of articulation, you'll have to make every movement count. Can you make it tilt up and down using some hidden putty? Can it waggle back and forth or side to side? You may be surprised by how much personality you can get out of a solid piece. Check out the film *Greedy Bricks* by Mirko Horstmann for a shining example of nonarticulated LEGO character animation.

These characters are limited by both articulation and copyright.

Practice, People-Watch, and Experiment

While we covered a lot in this chapter, our list of minifigure movements is far from complete. If you want to animate something complex like a backflip or breakdancing, here are some tips to keep in mind.

As we mentioned earlier, the best animators are great people-watchers. Think about the actions you want your minifigs to do, and consider how people perform those moves. Try watching yourself do the action in front of a mirror, or record a video of a friend doing it. You can also browse YouTube to find a video that shows the movement you want.

These are the main things to keep in mind: Which moments in the action are the most important? Which poses would translate well to a minifig? Grab a minifig and try posing it. Take some notes, draw some sketches, and then try it for real in front of the camera.

When planning out a character's performance, it's helpful to try acting it out yourself.

3 Animation Principles

Animation is a weird science.

You can think of Disney's "Nine Old Men" as the animation equivalent of the LEGO Group's Master Builders.

As with any skill, animation has its own time-tested standards to follow for best results. The original *Principles of Animation* were developed by the Walt Disney Company's "Nine Old Men," the expert artists who brought animation to the big screen for over half a century.

Two of the Nine—Frank Thomas and Ollie Johnston—collected their principles into a book called *The Illusion of Life*. In addition to being a nifty title for a book, the illusion of life is essentially every animator's goal: to make an audience believe that inanimate drawings, objects, or computer renderings have a spirit and a soul all their own.

The principles are centered on several important concepts:

- **Physics:** The study of how objects move through space and interact with each other. Your animated world will be more believable if the characters and objects behave according to real-world rules of gravity, friction, and so on. (We hope you stayed awake during science class.)

- **Clarity:** Making sure that whatever you're putting onscreen is straightforward and easy to understand. The most fluid animation in the world won't be worth a hill of beans if it's not presented clearly to the audience.

- **Engagement:** Keeping your audience's interest regardless of the content. Viewers don't have to like what you're showing them, but they should feel compelled to keep following along.

Even though the principles were conceived as guidelines for hand-drawn animation, most can be applied to any medium—including brickfilms. We've chosen the most relevant principles to highlight here, and we've added a few other tenets we found particularly pertinent to the craft of LEGO animation.

Exaggeration

Some folks will watch a great piece of animation and say, "Wow! That looks so *realistic*." While it may be flattering, this compliment is usually inaccurate. The animator's objective is not to make things look *real* but to make them look *alive*. The word *animation* literally means "the state of being full of life."

With that in mind, let's start with the principle of *exaggeration*. When you exaggerate your animation, you push a basic movement, pose, or feeling to its extreme. Actions, emotions, facial expressions, and attitudes all become overemphasized, creating a *caricature* of reality as opposed to an exact copy of it.

If a character is sad, exaggeration will make them *really* sad—hunched over with a big frown, drooping arms, and a slow, shuffling walk. If a character is happy, then they're *really* happy—full of boundless energy, arms a-flailin', and sporting the widest smile you've ever seen.

Exaggeration is especially helpful with minifigure animation, since (as we saw in Chapter 2) their articulation is limited and doesn't reflect human posability. When your character can't move the same way a living being does, you can compensate by exaggerating what movements they *can* do.

When creating a caricature, you take a subject's most distinct qualities and dial them up to 11. It's more about capturing a feeling than it is about accurate, realistic reproduction.

Exaggeration!

Exaggeration can make jolly pirates really jolly and sad clowns even more miserable.

Exaggeration can also change the energy of a whole scene. In this example, the main action is a character firing a projectile weapon.

If we exaggerate this main action, we can give the impression that the weapon being fired has enough power to knock the soldier backward.

We can also exaggerate the action in an unexpected way and surprise both the character and the audience.

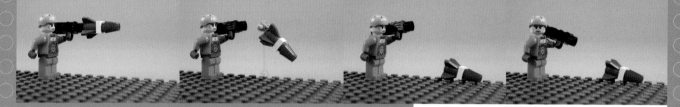

Don't be afraid to play around with exaggeration and see how far you can push your animation!

HOW MUCH EXAGGERATION IS TOO MUCH? THAT DEPENDS ON YOUR PERSONAL TASTE, BUT WHEN I'M ON SET, I SOMETIMES HEAR MY COLLEGE PROFESSOR'S VOICE ECHOING IN MY HEAD: "WHEN YOU THINK YOU'VE GONE FAR ENOUGH, GO FURTHER."

I APPLY THE PRINCIPLE OF EXAGGERATION TO EVERY PART OF MY FILMS, FROM SET DESIGN TO SOUND EFFECTS. I ENCOURAGE OUTRAGEOUS VOCAL PERFORMANCES BY TELLING MY VOICE ACTORS, "THERE'S NO SUCH THING AS OVER THE TOP." WHEN WRITING MY SCRIPTS, I PUSH MYSELF TO COME UP WITH THE SILLIEST IDEA POSSIBLE— AND THEN MAKE IT EVEN SILLIER.

THE JOY OF ANIMATION IS THAT YOU AREN'T LIMITED TO WHAT'S POSSIBLE . . . THE ONLY LIMIT IS YOUR IMAGINATION!

Squash and Stretch

In addition to exaggerating the movements and performances of your characters, you can also exaggerate their shapes. The principle of *squash and stretch* involves distorting the form of an object or character in order to add flexibility and a feeling of weight.

Yes, most LEGO elements are solid plastic shapes. But we've already seen some ways to get around this: the head pop and double-take from Chapter 2 are great examples of the squash and stretch principle in minifigure form. The individual minifig parts don't change, but the overall shape of the character does.

You can also squash and stretch using replacement animation—design a series of varying LEGO shapes and swap them out for interesting results. The shapes can get as crazy or weird as you want; the only thing that needs to remain constant is the *volume* of the entire construction. It should not look like the *size* of the form is changing, just the shape.

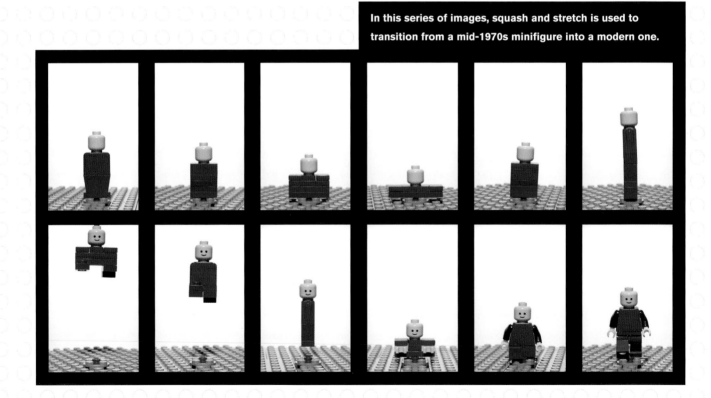

In this series of images, squash and stretch is used to transition from a mid-1970s minifigure into a modern one.

Exercise: Ball Bounce

One of the most classic animation examples is the bouncing ball. How do you get flat, plastic LEGO builds to look like a squishy ball? We've set it up for you frame-by-frame using a series of brick-built shapes. The main shape is the perfectly round ball (A); the others are either stretched (B, C) or squashed (D).

Build these simple shapes and re-create our ball-bounce animation. We animated this exercise with the camera pointed directly down at the animation surface. Notice where the shapes change from being perfect circles to squashed or stretched ellipses: the stretches happen on the faster parts of the bounce, and the squashes happen when the ball hits the ground.

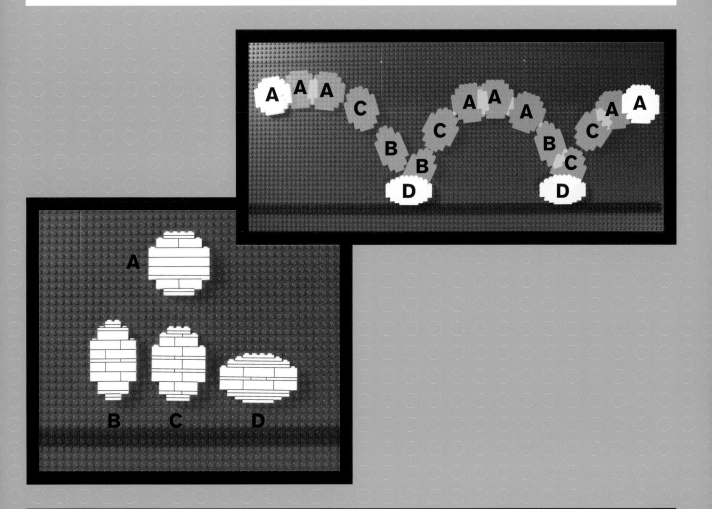

Timing and Spacing

Having completed the ball-bounce exercise, you may be wondering: How do you figure out how many frames each bounce should take? And what determines how far the ball needs to move between each frame?

Timing is the number of frames it takes to complete any given action. Fast movements require fewer frames, while slow movements require more. Animating a quick drive from point A to point B may require only 2 or 3 frames, but if you want to slow that movement down, you might need 10 or more frames to complete the same action.

Spacing is how far the object moves between each frame in order to complete the action. For slow-moving objects, the changes from frame to frame should be very tiny. Fast-moving objects will need to cover more distance between each frame.

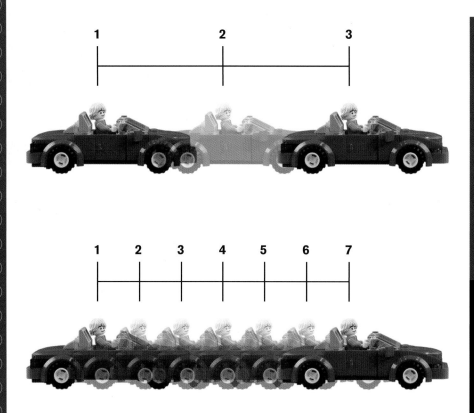

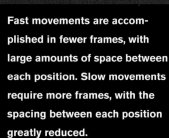

Fast movements are accomplished in fewer frames, with large amounts of space between each position. Slow movements require more frames, with the spacing between each position greatly reduced.

As with exaggeration, spacing can evoke a feeling or convey the energy of a scene to the audience, like the difference between a car cruising along slowly and a car roaring down the road.

Sometimes, the timing of an animation can stay the same while the spacing changes. In these examples, the car moves from left to right with the same timing (5 frames) but different spacing (the physical positions of the car).

With objects like cars, you'll probably have a pretty clear idea of what their speed should be (fast). But how quickly should a minifigure move? What about a falling rock or a robot dragon? The key to determining the speed of your animation is to think about the object's *weight*. Heavier things move slowly and require more frames to get from one position to another. Using timing and spacing to give the appearance of weight is critical for making an audience believe that your animated objects are moving on their own.

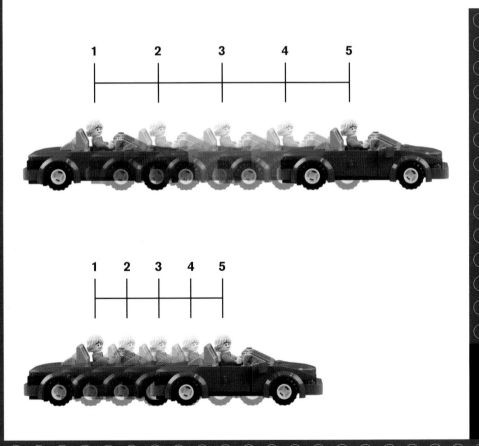

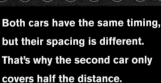

Both cars have the same timing, but their spacing is different. That's why the second car only covers half the distance.

Easing

Easing is another great way to add weight to your animation. It's a spacing technique that helps you adjust the speed of your animated objects, making them move in ways that are a bit more true to life.

Physical objects rarely move at a constant rate; they speed up and slow down depending on factors like their size and environment. Grab a 2×4 brick and start flicking it around your animation surface. You'll notice that the brick doesn't move in constant, equal amounts but decelerates (slows down) due to friction.

This concept can easily translate into animated actions. In the examples below, the car doesn't go from 0 to 60 miles per hour in an instant. It starts out slow and then takes a bit of time to reach top speed; that's *easing out* of the first position. If the driver hits the brakes, the car won't immediately stop in place; it'll slow down and then come to a stop, *easing in* to the last position.

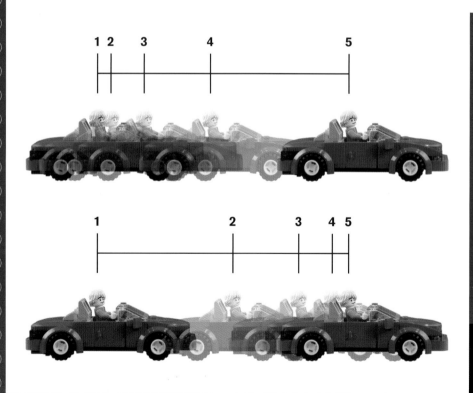

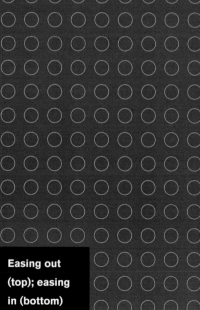

Easing out (top); easing in (bottom)

Easing can also inform something as basic as a minifig arm lift. As the arm is raised, the motion starts out slow, implying the heaviness of the limb and resistance from gravity. Then the arm starts to pick up speed—if the minifigure had muscles, this is where they would really kick in. (Take that, gravity!) As the arm approaches the end position, it slows down again before coming to a stop.

The best way to get a sense of weight and speed is through observation. We recommend watching your favorite movies with your thumb on the remote's slow-motion button to see how many frames a given action takes and how far objects move in order to complete that action. You can also record your own live-action videos and watch through them frame by frame.

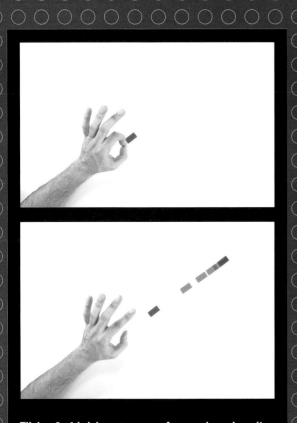

Flick a 2×4 brick across a surface and see how it slows down.

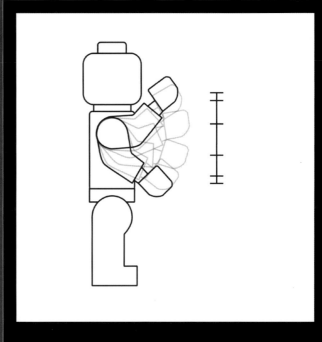

Easing can be used to add weight and nuance to minifig gestures.

Exercise: Pendulum Animation

Let's look at timing, spacing, and easing through a classic example: a swinging pendulum. We shot this flat on our animation surface with the camera pointing straight down at the tabletop.

The pendulum bob starts out on one side (1), at rest, but then accelerates in a downward arc. At the bottom of the arc (4), the pendulum is moving at its fastest. Then, as the bob reaches the other side, gravity starts to slow it down again. The bob pauses briefly at the extreme (7) before starting to swing back in the other direction.

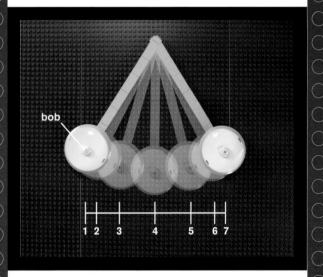

Try animating a pendulum of your own, using this image as a reference. Pay close attention to how the spacing of the bob changes depending on how fast it's supposed to be moving.

Anticipation, Follow-Through, and Recovery

Anticipation, as the name suggests, is the preparation for an action. Not only does it allow the character or object to get ready, but also it signals to the audience, "Pay attention! Something is about to happen." An anticipation can be big or small, subtle or obvious. It can be a long and drawn-out warm-up before your character performs or a simple glance off to the side before they take their exit.

Imagine someone pitching a ball. The pitcher doesn't just raise their arm and the ball flies away; they *prepare* for throwing the pitch by winding up first. That wind-up is the anticipation.

Once the pitcher has completed the action of throwing the ball, their body does not immediately stop dead; the pitcher will keep moving in the same direction that the pitch was thrown. This continued momentum immediately following an action is known as *follow-through*.

Finally, all of the body parts catch up to one another as the pitcher resumes an upright stance and settles into a neutral pose. This regaining of composure is called *recovery*.

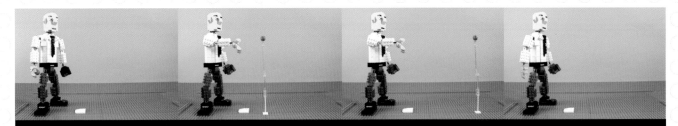

This pitcher raises his arm suddenly and the ball just goes—not very true to life.

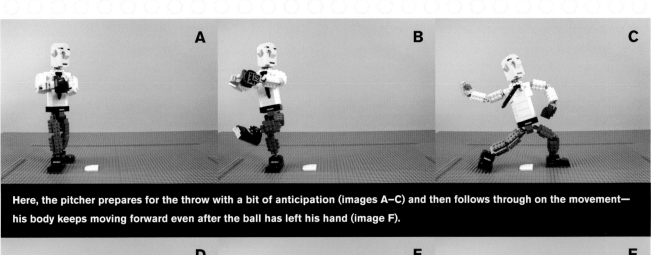

A B C

Here, the pitcher prepares for the throw with a bit of anticipation (images A–C) and then follows through on the movement—his body keeps moving forward even after the ball has left his hand (image F).

D E F

Arcs

In the natural world, things rarely move in perfectly straight lines. Animals, planets, and leaves in the wind all tend to follow *arcs*. Take a look back at the ball-bounce exercise—it's a perfect way to see arcs at work. Even someone walking forward in a straight line has an arc to their movement, as they bob up and down with each step.

But what shape should an arc be? Tall and narrow? Wide and shallow? Slow-moving objects have big, round arcs. Fast-moving objects have flatter arcs that are almost straight lines.

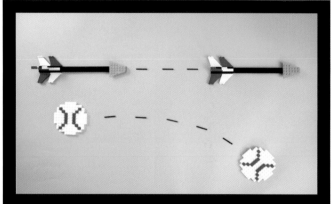

Compared to fast-moving objects (which move in arcs that are almost straight lines), slow-moving objects will eventually move downward in a more curved arc.

A leaf in the wind may swoop and glide, but it will always follow arcs.

Fortunately, minifigures have plenty of built-in arcs. You can see these almost instantly when moving an individual minifig's arm or head. But when those minifigures interact with props or move through their environment, keep an eye on their arcs.

Anna's minifigure joints make the arc of her wand waving smooth and easy to accomplish.

Exercise: Minifigure Jump

Let's put these principles into practice by making a mini-figure jump forward.

A. Start your minifig in a neutral pose.
B. Have the minifig *anticipate* their jump by leaning forward and swinging their arms back. Push those arms as far back as they can go—*exaggerate* the movement.
C. Over the next couple of frames, the minifig should quickly swing their arms forward and start straightening their body as they leave the ground.
D. As the character leaps forward, make sure they follow a nice *arc* up to the high point of their jump. The top of the jump is a great place to add *squash*—curl the minifig into a compact shape.

E. On the way down, keep the minifigure's arms raised and continue the arc as their body straightens out again in anticipation of the landing. (Note that the hat has lifted off of the character's head, adding a bit of *stretch*.)
F. Once they land, have the minifigure *follow through* on the jump by leaning them forward and bringing their arms down a few frames later. Even though the jump is complete, the body is still moving.
G. Finish the movement by having the minifig *recover*, and bring their body back up to a neutral pose.

Unlike the numbered diagrams, examples with lettered steps represent poses and not single frames of animation. Use your judgment to determine how many frames it should take to get from one pose to the next.

Overlapping Action

For each scene you create, you'll have at least one main action that your character needs to accomplish. As we saw in Chapter 2, those actions are generally built out of smaller movements. Suppose the main action of your scene is "two characters high-five each other." We can break down the characters' movements like this:

A. Start the characters in neutral poses.
B. Turn their heads to look at each other.
C. Turn their bodies toward each other.

D. Lean them forward to anticipate the action.
E. Lift their arms.
F. Lean them back.
G. Bring their arms toward each other.
H. Lean them forward.
I. Connect their hands—high five achieved!

If your characters were robots, they might perform each movement separately, like a list of programmed commands: *Complete first movement; stop. Complete second movement; stop.*

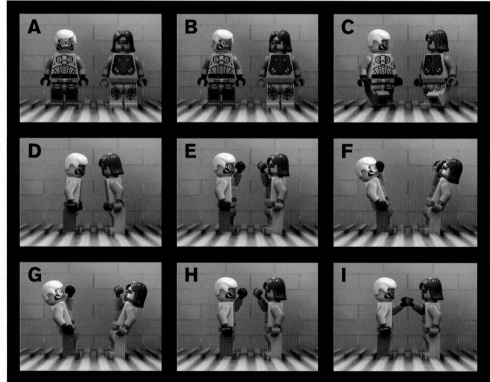

Their movements are mechanically accurate, but Annabot and Mattron don't quite capture the enthusiastic energy required for a high five.

But living beings wouldn't perform these movements one at a time. There would be *overlapping action*; some of the movements would happen simultaneously. This doesn't mean your characters need to do *everything* at once. Overlapping action is about finding a balance—staggering the moves so that only *some* of them happen at the same time.

Let's look at how living characters like Anna and Matt might high-five each other. First, they turn their heads and their bodies simultaneously, while also leaning forward to anticipate the high five. Then, as they raise their arms, they lean back. Finally, Anna and Matt lean their bodies toward each other. When they're done leaning forward, their arms keep moving downward as they slap their hands together in the universal sign of friendship and success.

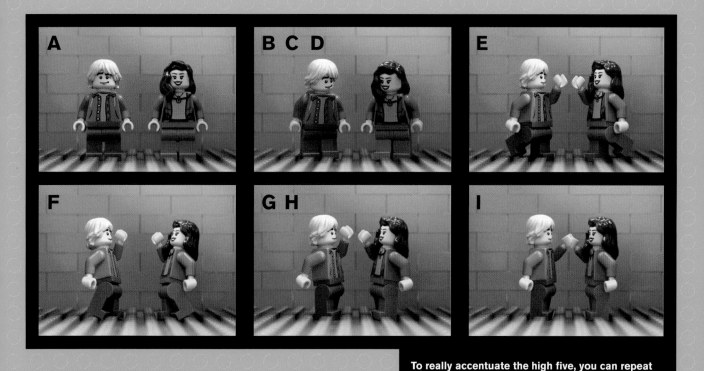

To really accentuate the high five, you can repeat the second-to-last pose (G H) after their hands connect. Up top!

Overlapping action adds depth and complexity to your animated performances. If you're transitioning between multiple minifigure gestures, overlapping can help smooth the movements out into one continuous motion. It can also be used to add follow-through: you can overlap a minifigure's body movements so that the head and arms move a few frames after the torso moves. When overlapping the action on a character's body, think of it as a kind of chain reaction: one part of the character will move first, and the others will follow through.

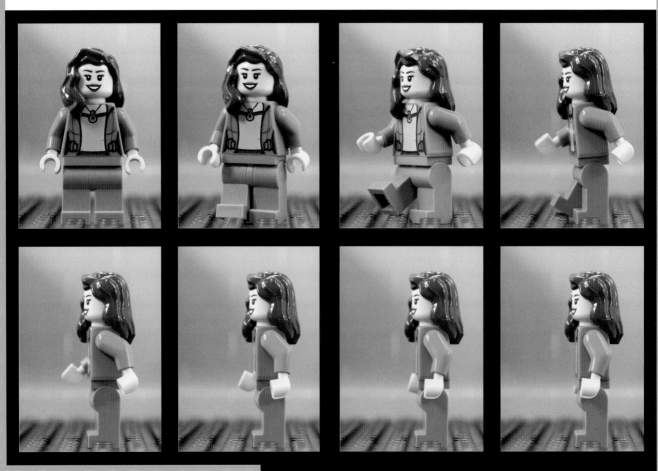

As Anna turns her body to the side, her arms follow. Once her body has stopped turning, the arms keep moving for a few frames to catch up.

Secondary Action

Now that you've seen how to layer movements with overlapping action, you can add even *more* complexity by introducing a *secondary action*. Secondary actions are additional flourishes that support a main action. They aren't critical to the execution of the main action, but they can help add variety and interest to otherwise unremarkable activities.

Let's take another look at one of the most common main actions: walking. By itself, there isn't much to a walk; you put one foot in front of the other and repeat as necessary. But if the main action is "a character is walking," a secondary action might be them carrying a tray of snacks as they walk. Or juggling. Or simply swinging a briefcase.

Even the arm movement as the character walks could be considered a secondary action. The main action—walking—can still happen without this, but it would be far less interesting to watch.

Secondary actions give Anna a new way to walk, and it makes her spirit shine.

As with overlapping action, you can also add follow-through using secondary actions. If your minifigure's main action is "shaking their head," a bald character could certainly get the point across. But why not add a secondary action: hair movement! Give the character hair and have them shake their head, but keep the hair moving separately a few frames after the head movement.

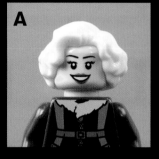
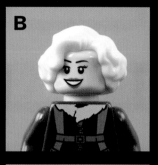

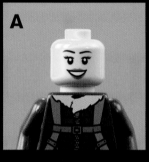
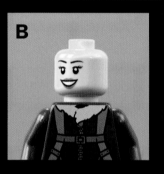
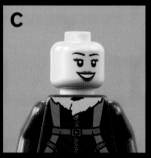
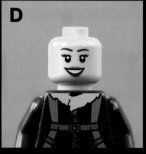

These bald head positions create a perfectly functional head shake, but add a hair piece and some follow-through, and va-va-voom! Instant shampoo commercial.

Or, if there's a superhero whose main action is "jumping down into the scene," add the secondary action of a billowing cape. Now, the cape can settle into place a few frames after the action of the character jumping down into the scene, adding both lifelike follow-through and a decorative touch.

Secondary actions are great for adding interest, but they shouldn't take center stage. If you can use them to spice up a performance, great! But if they're causing the main action to become muddied or confusing, you should probably cut them out. Animation is a form of communication, and clarity is key.

While he may be able to stop crime, this hero could be confused for a normal citizen dressed in a leotard.

Add billowy cape movement for some heroic follow-through flair.

Without clear staging, the furniture in this room would prevent viewers from experiencing the magic of *Sombearo*.

Staging and Blocking

Speaking of clarity, let's talk *staging*—setting up your animation in a way that is simple and straightforward. Unless you are deliberately trying to be confusing, your audience should always be able to follow what is happening.

If your scene is focusing on two characters, those characters should be front and center—not hidden behind a bush or obstructed by junk that prevents the camera (and thus, the viewer) from seeing the action. Get all of that clutter out of the way.

Sometimes, characters can even get in their own way. The minifigure is an elegant design, but it doesn't look great from every angle. One helpful way to double-check your staging is to imagine your characters as shadows. If you could only see a silhouette of your character, would their performance be clear? Posing your minifigures with strong silhouettes is a great way to keep their actions readable.

If a character is pointing, position them so the audience can clearly see their hand.

Also, be mindful of things like color—if a character wearing light blue stands in front of a light blue background, they can blend in and get lost.

Contrasting colors help your characters stand out from their background.

In addition to keeping things simple and direct for your audience, you should make things easy for yourself as the animator. The *blocking* of a scene is where you set up the paths of the action and place your characters, props, and vehicles in locations where they can do what they need to do.

Let's look at a scene where the main action is "character walks over to the table to grab their coffee mug." If the furniture in the room is haphazardly placed, the character has to take a long and winding path to get from the door to the table.

To simplify the action, keep your characters' paths easily walkable and free of obstructions. This can help you save time, both in the animation process and in the actual running time of your film (as well as saving your audience from confusion or boredom).

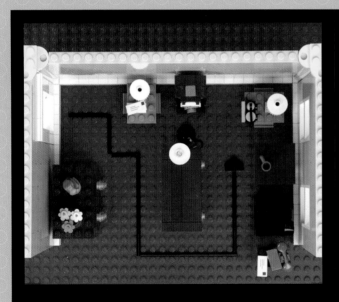

Somebody call an interior designer! This cluttered room is a feng shui nightmare.

Here, the path from the door to the coffee mug is much more direct. Adding a diagonal plate makes it easier for the character to walk at an angle.

Place your props where your characters can easily reach them.

Blocking also involves positioning characters, props, and vehicles where they can serve their intended purposes. In order to have a character pick up a coffee mug, for example, you need to put that coffee mug in the scene to begin with, and in a location where the character can reach it.

Finally, be aware of your character's physical limitations. If there's not enough room in your set, your character might not be able to perform to their full ability. Your character won't be physically able to pick up the mug if they are forced to stand too close to the table.

It's a good idea to think through your staging and blocking before animating—or even as early as when you're creating storyboards (Chapter 7) or composing your shots (Chapter 8). For now, just remember: simple is good.

Matt's reach is limited when he stands too close to the table. Adding one stud width of space leaves enough room for him to raise his arm and reach the coffee mug.

Trial and Error

Finally, we come to *trial and error*. This concept is not one of the original animation principles but rather the process by which the principles were developed. How do you know if something will work? You just have to try it and see how it goes. Once again, science comes into play—this time, the *scientific method*, in which you do the following:

- **Make observations:** We've already talked about how animators need to develop good people-watching skills, but it's more than that—look at how anything and everything moves in the natural world. When you drop something, how does it impact the ground? When somebody gets scared, what does their body do? Pay attention, take notes, and draw sketches.
- **Ask questions:** Don't be afraid to ask questions. If you're not sure how something would look or move or work, do research or ask other people before you dive in blindly. Chances are that someone else has wondered the same thing, and they might already have answers or results you can use.
- **Experiment:** The most direct way to learn is by doing. "I think this is how a dog might walk; let me try it out." Start small, and work your way up—before starting on your cinematic magnum opus, test out a character doing jumps or whatever weird animation bits you think your film will need. As we've said before, you shouldn't just read this book. Fire up your camera and follow along with our examples, or animate some tests of your own. The sets for your animation tests don't have to look pretty—they

just need to help you figure out how the animation will work.

- **Review the results:** Did your tests come out the way you thought they would? Great! Did they come out totally bizarre and not work at all? Also great! Making mistakes is one of the best ways to get better at something. Don't get caught up in the fear of failure—embrace it. Getting familiar with what doesn't work makes it easier to figure out what does. Just sit back down and try it again.

The principles of animation are kind of abstract, which is why there's no substitute for just trying things out. That's how both amateurs and pros improve. It might feel like you'll never stop learning some of these, but that's kind of the point. Practice doesn't really make perfect, but it can get you darn close.

> I USE EVERY PROJECT AS AN EXCUSE TO TRY SOMETHING NEW: "LET'S TRY A THREE-LEGGED ROBOT WALK," OR "HOW DO WE ANIMATE A SCENE THAT LOOKS LIKE IT WAS SHOT UNDERWATER?"

> SOMETIMES THE FINAL PRODUCT IS NOT AS GOOD AS I WANT IT TO BE, BUT I LEARN FROM THESE EXPERIMENTS AND PUT THAT KNOWLEDGE TOWARD THE NEXT PROJECT.

4 Building for Brickfilms

Building for animation isn't quite the same as building for play or display. You'll want your animation sets to be stable but versatile, feature impressive construction techniques, and still have space for your characters to move around.

Fortunately, this doesn't mean you'll need to build the entire world your movie takes place in. Just like on real film sets, buildings can be mere facades, cars can speed along with the help of moving backgrounds, and production tools can be hidden in plain sight. In this chapter, we'll show you all of these methods and more.

Building Stable Sets

Set bumps are no joke. Stop-motion is all about making, tiny, precise movements between frames, and even the slightest hiccup can undo hours of work. There are a few post-production tricks you can use to smooth out your set bumps, but the best solution is to avoid them entirely by building a stable set.

When we set up our animation workspace in Chapter 1, we talked about keeping all of the production equipment locked in place. This approach also extends to your movie sets. As you build your sets, props, vehicles, and characters, make sure that their parts will move only when *you* want them to. You are the director of your film, after all!

Make sure your animation set is stable. Otherwise, it could collapse during filming.

STOP-MOTION IS A PHYSICAL CHALLENGE. WHEN YOUR LIGHTS, CAMERA, AND SETS ARE CRAMPED TOGETHER, IT CAN BE TOUGH TO AVOID KNOCKING THINGS OVER.

DON'T STRESS OUT IF YOU HAVE A SET BUMP OR TWO IN YOUR ANIMATION. EVEN WHEN I HAVE A BIG SET BUMP, I JUST KEEP MOVING FORWARD.

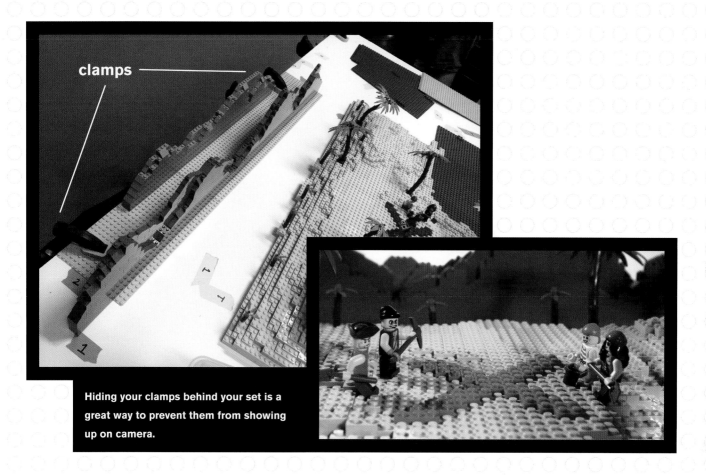

clamps

Hiding your clamps behind your set is a great way to prevent them from showing up on camera.

Securing Your Baseplates

Fortunately, a key component for keeping your sets locked down is probably already in your building arsenal: the *baseplate*. LEGO baseplates give your brickfilm sets a flat foundation that sits flush with your animation surface. Baseplates also provide perfect floors for interior sets and are available in a variety of colors.

As you build your set, leave extra baseplate space at the edges so you can fasten the baseplate to your animation surface. If you're using masking tape, simply tape down the four corners of the baseplate. If clamps are more your style, you may need to build extensions onto your baseplate so that the whole foundation reaches the end of the table. No matter which approach you choose, make sure that your fasteners of choice are not visible to the camera.

Build firmly and carry a soft hammer.

Making Strong Connections

When building your sets, take full advantage of *clutch power*—the ability of every LEGO brick and element to stick together. As you build, double-check your stud connections to make sure that they're tight, and use locking or stair-stepping techniques so that none of the pieces will pop off.

Make sure your models are tightly connected to your baseplate, too. You can use a small rubber mallet to lightly tap a build onto a baseplate, ensuring a secure connection.

Securing Unstable Elements

In general, you should avoid using these unstable elements in your film sets:

- Wheels, propellers, and anything else that spins freely
- Tree and plant elements that don't attach fully
- Rubbery hair pieces
- Nonfriction Technic pins
- Sections of official LEGO kits that are designed to be easily removed for play

If you really need to include these elements, you can use sticky tack or putty to attach them firmly.

"Loose Man" really wanted to be in *The Magic Picnic*, but he was too unstable to animate.

Sticky tack is perfect for securing objects with no viable stud connections. When placed just right, it's barely visible to the camera.

Testing Your Set

Once you've got your set arranged how you want it, it's time to make your final checks. Can your hands reach comfortably into the parts of the set you need to animate in? Are there any dangly bits that you might hit while moving around your set? Questions like these may not come up until you start shooting, but the sooner you can verify the security of your set pieces, the better.

Building for Movement

There will be times when the things you've built will need to bend, rotate, or disconnect entirely. In these instances, it's once again important that *you* are the one determining when and how your sets move.

Articulation

When we talk about articulation, we're usually talking about character flexibility. Minifigures have articulated arms, legs, necks, and hands. But your movie sets can be articulated, too.

Hinges, turntables, clips, pins, and ball-and-socket joints are all invaluable components for creating the articulated sections of your sets, props, and vehicles. These LEGO elements are made with movement in mind, and their various shapes, sizes, and colors allow for seamless integration into your models.

Hinges, Clips, and Bars

- **Best used for:** Movement that has a clear start and end point along one axis
- **Downsides:** Overly susceptible to gravity
- **Example uses:** Spaceship wings, creature mouths, aircraft landing gear

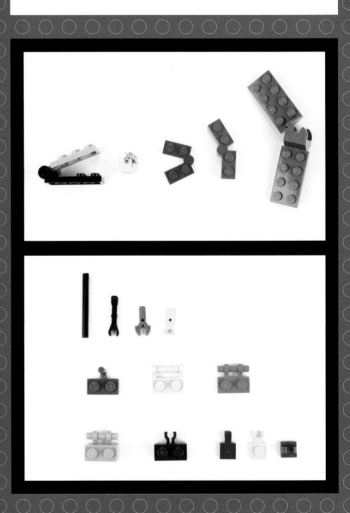

Turntables and Pins

- **Best used for:** Precise rotation around a single point
- **Downsides:** Looseness; unwanted movement is hard to avoid
- **Example uses:** Minifig-scale desk chairs; props that spin, swing, or hang; wheels on a bus

1 Using 1×1 round plates allows for rotation around a single point.

2

I USE ROUND 1X1 PLATES AS MAKESHIFT "TURNTABLES" WHENEVER I HAVE A CHARACTER SITTING IN A CHAIR. PLACING THE STUD INTO THE TUBE ON THE BOTTOM OF THE CHAIR GIVES A NICE TIGHT CONNECTION BUT STILL ALLOWS THE CHAIR TO ROTATE 360 DEGREES.

Ball-and-Socket Joints

- **Best used for:** Free, exact movement along multiple axes
- **Downsides:** Can be tough to track arcs or keep aligned
- **Example uses:** Robot arms, dragon wings, off-screen supports for minifig characters

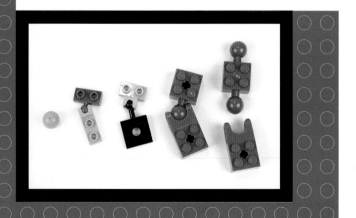

Click Hinges

Certain hinges and turntables lock into place with a "click." This limits the positions they can hold but adds a bit more stability. Click elements aren't great for precise movements, but if you need a joint that can hold its place at an angle or a turntable that can rotate exactly 360 degrees every couple of seconds, they just might do the trick.

With mech-type robots, click joints are often used in the legs for stability, while free-moving ball-and-socket joints give the arms greater posability.

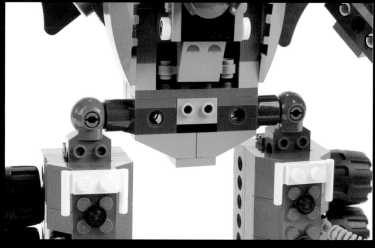

Disconnection

Now let's talk about building things that need to come apart or move during the animation process. Whether you're moving mountains or knocking down walls, there are techniques and approaches for every situation. The main elements of choice for disconnection are *offset plates* and *tiles*.

Offset Plates

Offset plates come in a few varieties. The most common versions of these elements are the 1×2 and 2×2, both of which have a single stud on top. This is great for a stud connection that's tight enough to hold something in place but not so tight that you can't easily remove it when necessary.

If there's a prop your character needs to pick up, you can attach it to an offset plate for the first part of the shot to keep it from moving around. When the time comes, the item will pop off easily so you can put it into your character's hands.

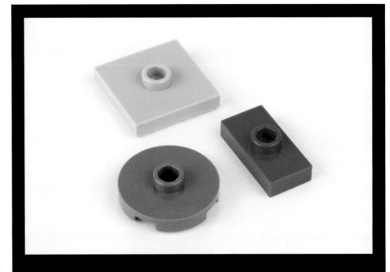

Offset plates hold things in place until it's time to move them.

Tiles

Use tiles in your set when you need something to slide. You can build a groove onto your baseplate, cover it with tiles, and then build the movable part of the set on top. Since LEGO tiles don't have studs, the portions you build on top will be constantly loose—but this means you can move them with greater precision.

Here's an example of a racetrack that uses this technique to make it look like the cars are speeding by. The checkerboard barriers, trees, and mountains in the background are each sitting in their own tiled channel. During animation, those parts are moved while the cars and camera stay still, giving the illusion of fast movement down the racetrack.

The fence, trees, and mountains can all slide because they're sitting on tiles.

Building for Versatility with Modular Sets

Your LEGO film sets are much tinier than real-life film sets. Your camera, however, is a normal, human-sized camera. So what can you do if your camera doesn't fit into the tiny spaces you've built for your film? Or if your hands don't fit?

Try building your sets as independent *modules*. You may be familiar with this concept from the LEGO Modular Buildings product line: each building in the series is a stand-alone module that can connect to the others. But these buildings are modular in more ways than one—they also have separate floors, which can be disconnected and recombined in a variety of ways. Let's take a look at how these two methods can inform your movie set designs.

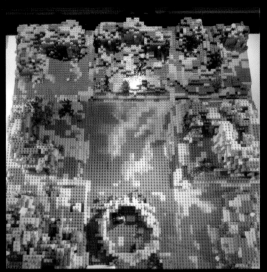

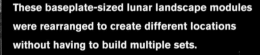

These baseplate-sized lunar landscape modules were rearranged to create different locations without having to build multiple sets.

You can build a whole bunch of modules that can be recombined into dozens of different sets, which is perfect for when you don't have a lot of bricks to work with. For example, you could create a few baseplate-sized chunks of a sandy beach, an underground cave, or the surface of some alien planet. Then, you can reuse and recombine them into a variety of arrangements and give viewers the illusion that the world you've built is much larger than it actually is.

Your modular sets can even be as simple as a single room. Let's say you need to film different angles of a scene inside that room. How do you get your camera inside without taking apart and rebuilding the whole set?

If you plan to get those camera angles from the very beginning, you can build a room that can be taken apart. Solid, whole chunks of wall that are sturdy (but can be easily removed and replaced later) will make animating inside your room much easier.

This is very similar to how some film and theater sets work. The walls in these kinds of modular sets are called *flats*. In live-action films and television shows, they are made to be moved, removed, and replaced, depending on where the lights, camera, and actors need to go.

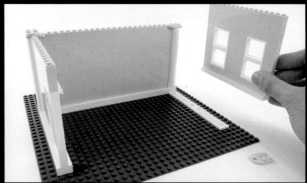

Offset plates and tiles allow the walls to be removed easily.

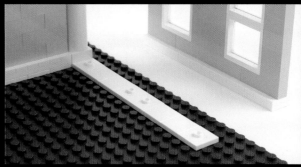

When the walls are in place, secure the top corners.

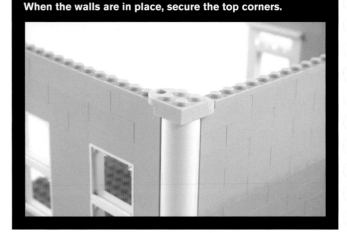

Exercise:
Build a One-Room Set

Try building a simple room, like this one from *The Magic Picnic*. It has only three walls (like on a TV sitcom), but we've built this set so we can easily snap different components in and out. (Notice how tiles and offset plates are used to attach the walls to the base.)

You want to make sure your set is sturdy enough to stay in place during the actual animation but not so unbelievably solid that the individual sections can't be removed or replaced easily when necessary.

This scene originally called for a narrow hallway, but the wizards at Paganomation transfigured it into a spacious stairwell to allow for easier animation.

ANOTHER APPROACH IS TO DESIGN YOUR SETS TO BE AS SPACIOUS AS POSSIBLE. YOUR STORY MIGHT CALL FOR A NARROW HALLWAY, BUT YOU CAN REWRITE THE SCENE TO TAKE PLACE IN AN OPEN AREA—ONE THAT WILL ACCOMMODATE BOTH YOUR CAMERA AND HANDS.

SOMETIMES, ADAPTING YOUR STORY TO FIT THE SET DESIGN IS A MORE EFFECTIVE SOLUTION.

Brick-Built Special Effects

In addition to characters, sets, and vehicles, you can also use LEGO pieces to build *special effects*. For our purposes here, special effects include:

- Lasers
- Fire
- Smoke
- Explosions
- Muzzle flashes (the burst of light from a projectile weapon being fired)

- Environmental and atmospheric effects (water, rain, snow, clouds, lightning, and so forth)

Many brickfilmers add these things to their movies in post-production as computer-generated effects. But this is the *LEGO Animation Book*, not the *Add CG Stuff After the Fact Book*. If it can be done with LEGO bricks and elements, why not do it?

What do this wave and this shattering window have in common? They're both made out of LEGO pieces!

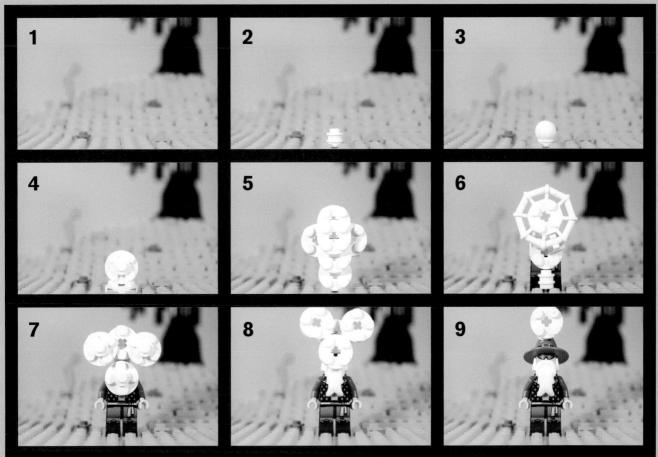

Exercise: Up in Smoke

Here's one way to build a pretty sweet smoke explosion using replacement animation. We built separate stages of an explosion cloud and swapped out the different pieces in between each frame. We also added in the wizard's body parts one frame at a time to help sell the illusion of his magical appearance. Real explosions are quick, so the final animation lasts less than one second.

We used this smoke explosion to make a wizard appear, but it can be used for many situations.

The hill where Matt and Anna have their picnic is all by itself—it's not part of a larger landscape.

Build What the Camera Sees

This last brickfilm building tip is also the most important. With LEGO models that you want to show off or display, the goal is to make the coolest, most detailed creations possible. The typical MOC ("my own creation") is made to be seen in person by an audience, from all sides and all angles.

But most of those details wouldn't show up in a film. Your brickfilm sets will be seen from only a few specific camera angles. To make your life and animating easier, you should build *only* the elements that the camera will see.

The Magic Picnic's city shots take place in two locations: the picnic hillside and the microscale city where the final showdown happens. Rather than building the entire city, we built only a few different buildings. Some of the buildings have a different facade on the front and back so we could reverse and reuse them for different shots. Other buildings have no back at all.

This is how a lot of live-action film exteriors work. If you ever visit a studio backlot, you'll see many buildings are just facades. They imply a location that's much larger than it actually is. These backlot facades can be moved and altered to create the appearance of an entire city.

Building with reuse in mind is a great way to save time. The fronts and backs of these buildings are different, making it look like you've built six when you really built only three.

This building exists only as a facade—the back is hollow and unfinished, since it won't be visible to the camera.

Building only what the camera sees can involve some planning on your part. You'll need to figure out which parts of your scene will be visible in every shot of your film. It can be helpful to design your movie set with the camera turned on so that you can see how the set looks onscreen as you build it. If it looks good on camera, that's all that matters.

LEGO building and stop-motion animation can be long, difficult processes, and our time on this Earth is precious. So remember: anything that doesn't appear in front of the camera won't be seen by your audience. And if it isn't seen by your audience, there's no sense in taking the time to build it, no matter how impressive or cool it is. Make sure to show off all the cool stuff you create!

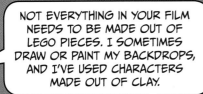

NOT EVERYTHING IN YOUR FILM NEEDS TO BE MADE OUT OF LEGO PIECES. I SOMETIMES DRAW OR PAINT MY BACKDROPS, AND I'VE USED CHARACTERS MADE OUT OF CLAY.

USE YOUR IMAGINATION AND TRY INCLUDING OTHER MATERIALS IN YOUR FILM.

5 Working in Different Scales

Is animating minifigs not enough of a challenge for you? You can mix things up by picking a different *scale* for your film sets and characters—that is, make them a whole different size. Building in different scales can add detail and scope to your brickfilms.

So far, everything in this book has been done in *minifigure scale*—meaning the sets, props, and vehicles are all sized to fit minifigures comfortably. The majority of LEGO kits and fan creations are built to minifigure scale. However, they represent just a small portion of the endless creative opportunities of the LEGO system.

So what other scales are possible? As with most LEGO building endeavors, there's an unlimited number of options. In this chapter, we'll cover a few common scales that you can use in your films.

Microscale

Microscale creations are a great way to convey vast landscapes and giant characters without using thousands of pieces. The challenge (and fun) of microscale is in shrinking items down to their smallest recognizable details. Can you build a convincing car with just 20 pieces? How about 2?

- **Strengths:** Requires fewer pieces than any other scale, focuses on the big picture
- **Weaknesses:** Characters lack expressiveness and articulation, tinier sets mean even more miniscule stop-motion movements
- **Example LEGO sets:** Mini Modulars (#10230), LEGO Architecture
- **Example brickfilms:** *Civilisation* by Jon Rolph (CheesyBricks), end credits from *The LEGO Movie*

Matt and Anna come face to face with their microscale counterparts.

Microscale creations (like these buildings) may look overly simplistic from certain angles, but remember: it's about what the camera sees while taking a picture, not about what you see while building.

A few familiar faces

Minifigure Scale

You know it, you love it, you've seen it throughout this book: *minifigure scale* is the tried-and-true standard of LEGO animation. What is it about these tiny characters—apart from being adorable and endlessly customizable—that makes animating them so intuitive? When it comes to brickfilming, we think their appeal is tied to their inherent limits.

With sophisticated animation puppets, you can easily get overwhelmed by the myriad ways to pose and position them. Minifigures, with their seven points of articulation, take a lot of the guesswork out of animation.

- **Strengths:** Lots of design options, easy to find
- **Weaknesses:** Limited articulation, small
- **Example LEGO sets:** Where do we even begin?
- **Example brickfilms:** *Minilife TV* by Christopher Salaises and *Henri & Edmond – Droits d'auteur* by Maxime Marion

"That's one small step for a Miniland astronaut, and one giant leap for us minifigs."

Miniland Scale

If you've ever been to a LEGOLAND theme park, you may already be familiar with *Miniland-scale* creations—so named for the area of the park they're displayed in. At 10 bricks tall, Miniland-scale figures are the next step up from minifigures.

Just because you're building in Miniland scale doesn't mean you have to follow the Miniland building standard, which has some specific guidelines. Instead, you can create your own characters that approximate the sizes of these figures and use other Miniland-scale builds as inspiration and reference. If there's one thing LEGO fans are good at, it's inspiring one another.

- **Strengths:** Small size, highly customizable, a world of reference material via LEGOLAND theme parks and books
- **Weaknesses:** Expressionless faces, accompanying film sets and props must be bigger
- **Example LEGO sets:** LEGO Store Monthly Mini Model Builds, LEGOLAND Entrance with Family (#40115)
- **Example brickfilms:** *Robota* by Marc Beurteaux, *Little Guys . . . in Space!* by Paganomation

Normal Miniland figures are designed to hold rigid poses, but you can modify them for animation. Create a few different posed limbs and swap them out using replacement animation, or add articulation using hinges, clips, and bars.

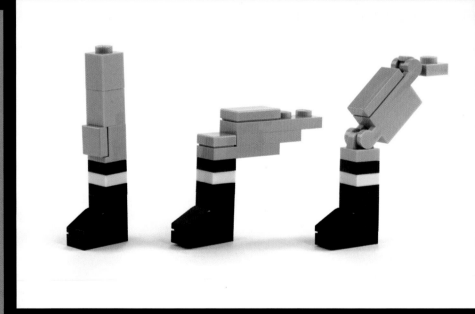

PaganoPuppets

As we mentioned in Chapter 4, certain LEGO bricks and elements—hinges, turntables, joints, and so on—can give your movie sets articulation. But you can also use these pieces to build your own large-scale, articulated animation puppets.

These animated figures have their origins in the Paganomation film *Playback* and have come to be known as *PaganoPuppets* (hat tip to Marc-André Caron for that name).

The PaganoPuppet can be highly detailed. As its main source of articulation, it uses large ball-and-socket joints, which provide an increased range of motion. But the bigger your characters get, the more you'll need to worry about how their weight can impact their mobility. Tie-downs will also become an issue—make sure there's enough clutch power between your character's feet and your film set to keep them upright and in place.

- **Strengths:** Greater articulation, facial animation is possible
- **Weaknesses:** Increased weight, accompanying film sets and props must be *way* bigger
- **Example LEGO sets:** None . . . yet
- **Example brickfilms:** *Plastic Giant* by Vacca Production, *Tout le bloc en parle* by Marc-André Caron

"Howdy, little partners! Have either of you seen a 4×2 in blue?"

PaganoPuppets are really great at standing in one spot. Running and jumping are a bit more difficult.

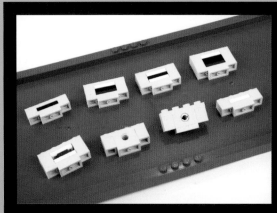

These mouth shapes were used in *Country Buildin'*.

The size of the PaganoPuppet does offer an advantage, though: it's big enough for brick-built lip sync. You can create different mouth shapes for your characters, which will allow you to do facial animation on set.

Puppet Building Instructions

Build your own PaganoPuppet! Every time these characters show up in a new Paganomation production, they get more and more intricate. Here's the latest version—the figure is presented as plainly as possible so that you can customize it to your heart's content. Maybe you can figure out other ways to adapt this puppet design into something even better! (See the bill of materials on page 106 or download a parts list from the book's website at *https://www.nostarch.com/legoanimation/*.)

Head

1 3x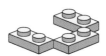

2 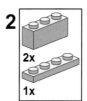 2x 1x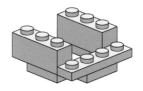

3 2x 1x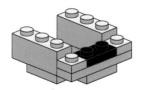

4 2x 1x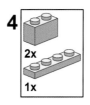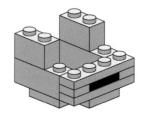

5 2x 1x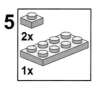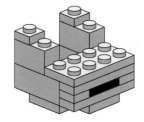

6

2x

2x

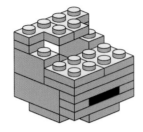

7

1x

1x

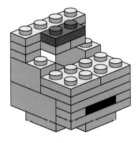

8

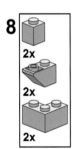

2x

2x

2x

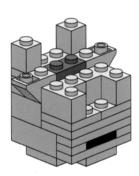

9

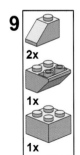

2x

1x

1x

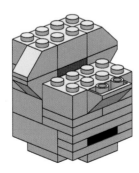

10

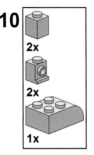

2x

2x

1x

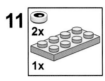

11

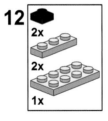

2x

1x

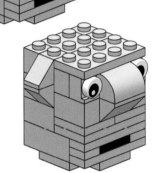

12

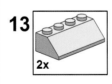

2x

2x

1x

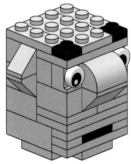

13

2x

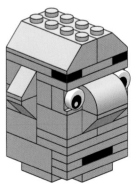

Neck

1

 1x

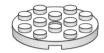

2

 1x
1x ③

3

1x
3x

4

1x

5

1x
1x
1x

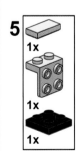

Torso

1

2x
1x

2

2x
1x
1x

3

1x
4x
1x 1x
1x 1x

4

2x

1x

2x

1x

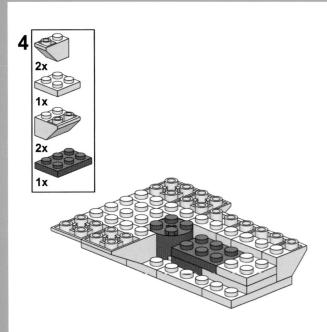

5

2x

2x

2x

1x   1x

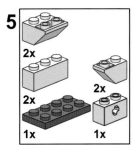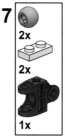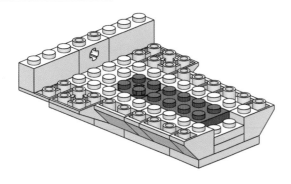

6

1x

2x

2x

2x   1x

1x

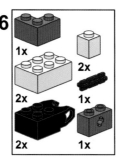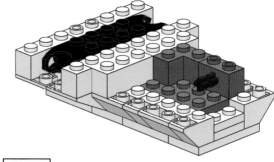

7

2x

2x

1x

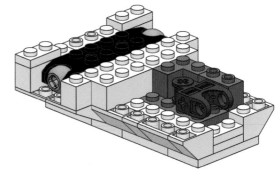

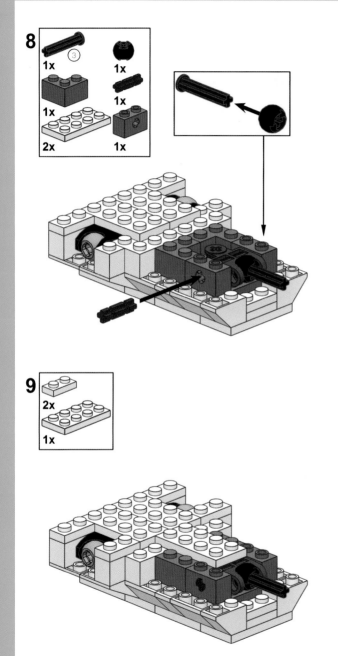

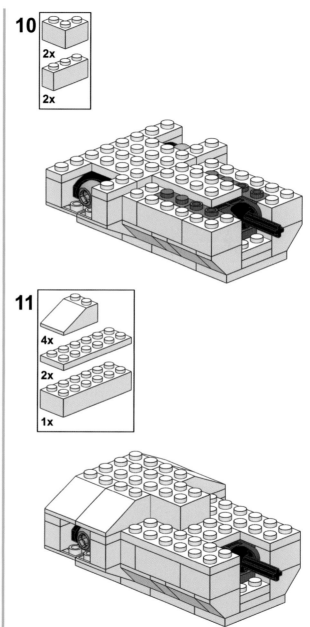

12

3x
1x

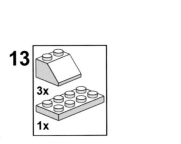

13

3x
1x

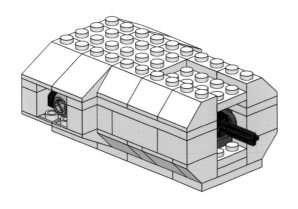

14

1x
1x
2x
1x

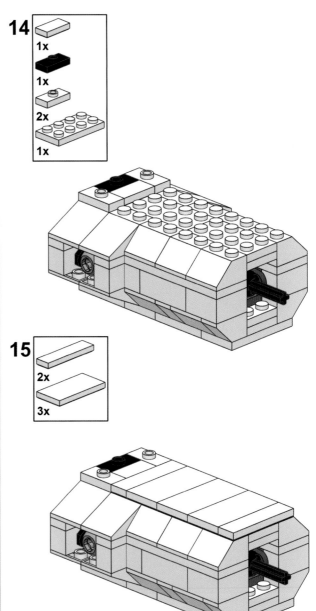

15

2x
3x

16

1x
2x

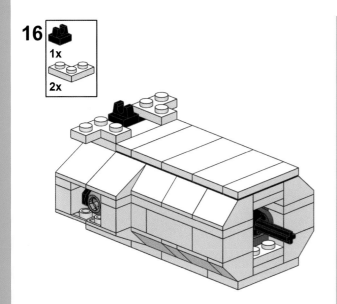

17

1x
1x

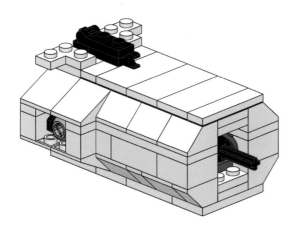

18

1x
1x
1x

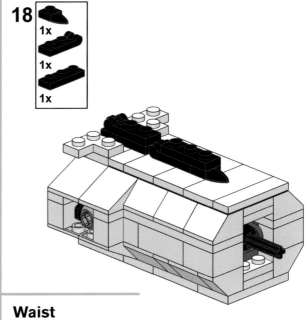

Waist

1

1x

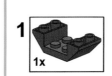

2

2x
1x

3

1x
1x

4

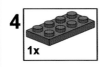

1x

5

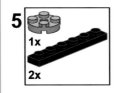

1x

2x

6

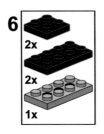

2x

2x

1x

 2x

7

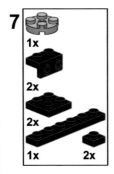

1x

2x

2x

1x   2x

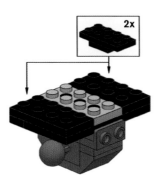

8

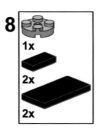

1x

2x

2x

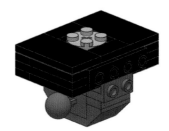

9

2x

1x

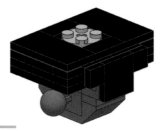

Upper Right Leg

1

1x

1x

2

1x

1x

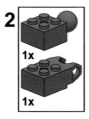

3

2x

2x

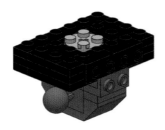

4

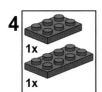 1x 1x

5

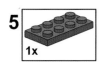 1x

Lower Right Leg

1

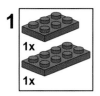 1x 1x

2

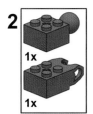 1x 1x

3

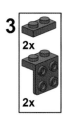 2x 2x

4

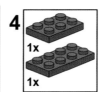 1x 1x

5

 1x 1x

6

 1x 1x

Upper Left Leg

1

 1x 1x

2

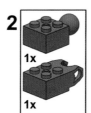 1x 1x

3

2x

2x

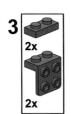 

4

1x

1x

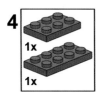 

5

1x

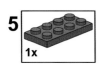 

Lower Left Leg

1

1x

1x

2

1x

1x

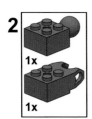 

3

2x

2x

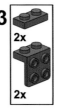 

4

1x

1x

5

1x

1x

6

1x

1x

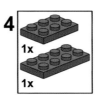 

Foot (2x)

1

2x

1x

 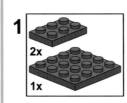 

2

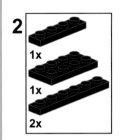 1x
1x
2x

3

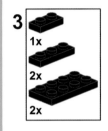 1x
2x
2x

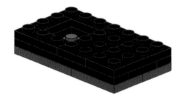

4

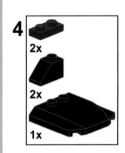 2x
2x
1x

5

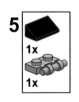 1x
1x

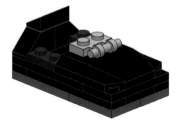

6

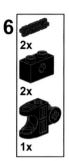 2x
2x
1x

1
2
3

7

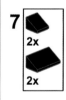 2x
2x

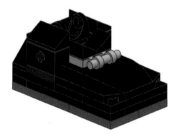

Upper Arm (2x)

1

 2x

2

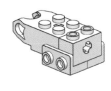 1x
1x

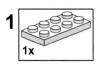

3

 1x
1x ③

4

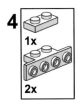 1x
2x

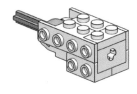

5

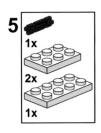 1x
2x
1x

 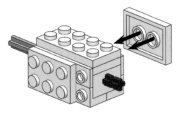

6

 1x

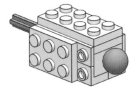

Lower Arm (2x)

1

1x

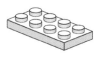

2

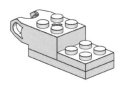 1x
1x

3

2x
1x
1x

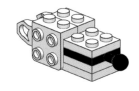

4

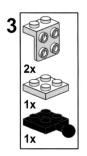 2x

5

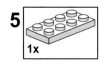 1x

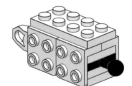

Left Hand

1
 1x
 1x

2
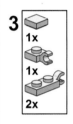 1x 1x

3
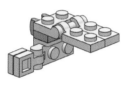
1x
1x
2x

4
2x
1x

5
2x
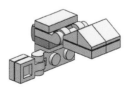

Right Hand

1
 1x 1x

2
 1x 1x

3
1x
1x
2x
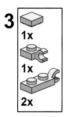

4
2x
1x
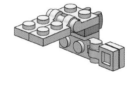

5
2x

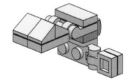

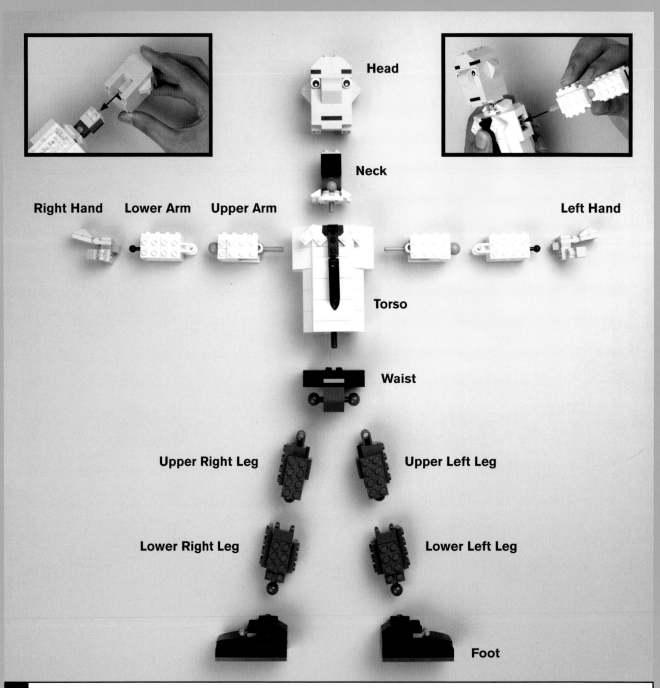

Head

Neck

Right Hand   Lower Arm   Upper Arm   Left Hand

Torso

Waist

Upper Right Leg   Upper Left Leg

Lower Right Leg   Lower Left Leg

Foot

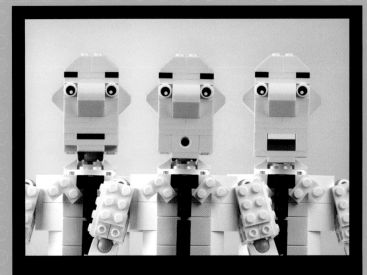

PaganoPuppets use replacement animation mouth shapes for lip sync.

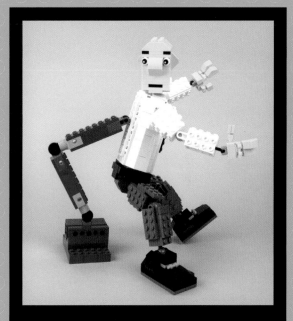

If your PaganoPuppet needs to pose in an off-balance way, build a support to hold them up.

Bill of Materials

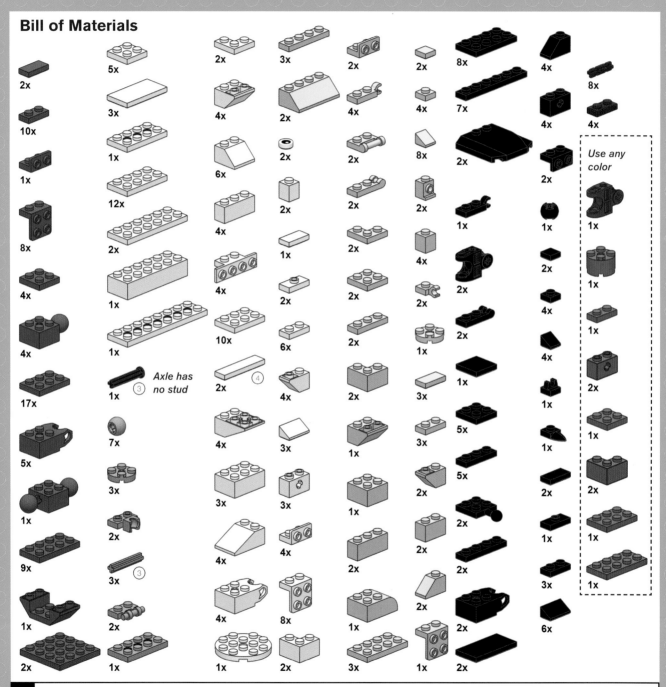

"Little Guys!" Scale

The other well-known Pagano scale comes from the *Little Guys!* films and features highly complex, expressive characters. These rigs are really more like articulated LEGO sculptures, and because of their scale, the characters are built only from the waist up. Even so, the amount of detail in their designs is unparalleled.

However, these puppets are the most susceptible to gravity. When working at *Little Guys!* scale, try not to go overboard with detail—added detail usually means added weight. Keeping your characters light will allow them to hold a pose long enough for you to take a picture. Making your characters' body parts as hollow as possible is another great way to minimize their weight.

- **Strengths:** Most intricate facial animation possible, huge levels of detail, wow factor
- **Weaknesses:** Heavy; ball-and-socket joint use is limited; animation is more cumbersome; requires a *lot* of bricks
- **Example brickfilms:** *Pokeballin 2* by Dylan Woodley, *MIMUS* by Steffen Troeger (golego animation)

"I hope she doesn't get hungry . . . "

Ironically, the *Little Guys!* scale is the largest scale in the book.

The cyborg on the left has a really cool beret. Unfortunately, it made her head so heavy that she became really difficult to animate.

Little Guys! scale allows for very expressive brick-built facial animation.

Other Scales

Remember: you're not limited to these scales. Even within the LEGO system, there are many other options to play with: Duplo, Belville, Mixels, Bionicle, and more. You can create and animate any characters you'd like—big, small, or in between!

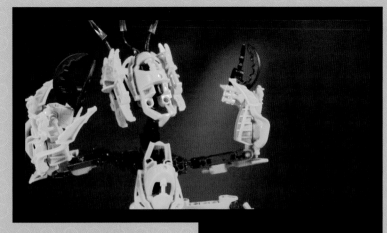

Bionicle characters and other "constraction" figures make great use of ball joints.

Belville and Technic figures offer more posability than minifigs.

MR. PAGANO LIKES TO BUILD HUMAN CHARACTERS OUT OF BRICKS, BUT I LIKE TO BUILD GIANT MONSTERS AND ROBOTS!

EVEN THOUGH THESE ARE LARGE CHARACTERS, THEY EXIST IN A MINIFIGURE WORLD, SO THEY ARE TECHNICALLY BUILT TO MINIFIGURE SCALE.

6 Tools of the Trade

Choosing animation equipment is a complex task with no one-size-fits-all answer. In order to pick what's right for you, you'll need to consider your budget, skill level, desired features, and computer operating system. Throughout this chapter, we'll help you make informed choices by discussing the strengths and weaknesses of all kinds of tools. Remember, having the right tool can make all the difference!

Fighting with an uncooperative camera isn't much fun.

Cameras

Choosing your camera is one of the most important decisions you'll make as an animator. Understanding camera options and features will save you from future headaches.

What to Look For

When you're searching for the perfect camera, here are some features to keep an eye out for.

Manual Settings

One important camera feature is manual control over image settings: focus, zoom, aperture, shutter speed, ISO, and white balance (more on these in Chapter 8). If you can't adjust these settings manually, then your camera is making decisions for you—which can result in blurry, inconsistent photos. If we've learned anything from science fiction, it's that letting machines make decisions for humans rarely ends well.

Power Supply

Make sure your camera has a power adapter so you can plug it into the wall instead of relying on battery power. If your camera has a power-saving auto-shutoff function, find out how to disable it. This will prevent your camera from turning off while you're in the middle of animating.

Macro Focus

Many cameras have a macro focus mode, which lets you focus on objects that are a few inches away from the camera lens. If your camera has interchangeable lenses, make sure one of them is a good macro lens.

Picture Resolution

Most modern cameras can take pictures at very high resolutions. Make sure that yours takes pictures at or above the resolution you want to use for your final product. A good baseline resolution for beginners is 1280×720 pixels, but advanced animators often shoot at 1920×1080 pixels or above. Remember: you can shrink a large picture later, but you can't enlarge a small picture and retain the same image quality.

Video Recording

Stop-motion animation uses still images, but sometimes it's useful to record live-action footage, so you might want to choose a camera that can also record video.

Remotes are a handy way to press a button from a distance.

Remote Control

Ideally, you should take pictures via a wired or wireless remote. This will prevent you from accidentally moving the camera when you're animating. Some animation software lets you control your camera through your computer, or you can buy a physical camera remote.

Storage Capacity

You'll be taking a lot of photos on your camera; 1 minute of stop-motion animation can easily contain 1,000 individual pictures. Make sure your camera (or its memory card) has enough storage for at least a few hundred high-resolution photos. For beginner and intermediate animators, 16GB of memory should be enough.

Software Compatibility

If you already have animation software, check to make sure that your camera is fully supported by that software. You can consult the software manufacturer for this information—for example, the website for Dragonframe (a fancy piece of software for pros) has a list of compatible cameras with detailed notes about what features each model can or can't use. See "Software and Hardware Compatibility" on page 131 for more information.

Budget

Camera prices range from less than $20 to over $2,000. Think about how much money you're willing to spend on a camera. If you're brand new to animation, we strongly recommend starting with a camera you already own.

As we'll discuss next, there are several categories of cameras you can choose from, so you're sure to find one that fits your particular budget.

NOTE *Equipment recommendations are color coded for easy reference:*

Blue = beginner
Green = intermediate
Orange = advanced

A smartphone is a great camera for beginners.

Smartphones and Tablets

If you already own a smartphone or tablet device, you can definitely use it for stop-motion—it's a great entry-level animation camera.

- **Strengths:** Portable, relatively inexpensive, can use all-in-one apps like Stop Motion Studio

- **Weaknesses:** Manual controls are limited or nonexistent, image resolution is low, exporting capabilities and remote-control options are limited
- **Recommended for:** Budget-conscious, first-time animators
- **We suggest:** If you already own one, use it to get your feet wet with stop-motion

Webcams

Webcams are a small, inexpensive option for brick-filmers. Their size makes it easy to get them eye level with your minifig actors, and they can be used with a variety of stop-motion software programs. Many brick-filmers swear by their webcams and never feel the need to pick up something more expensive.

- **Strengths:** Inexpensive, easy to use with stop-motion software, some can shoot high-definition (HD) resolutions, powered by the computer rather than batteries (so they won't turn off mid-shot)
- **Weaknesses:** Limited picture quality, no interchangeable lenses, require specialized software to unlock their full potential
- **Recommended for:** Mid-level animators looking for more control than a smartphone
- **We suggest:** Logitech Pro webcams (for example, the C920 or the QuickCam 9000)

Webcams are versatile and work well with stop-motion software.

A point-and-shoot camera can take high-quality photos.

Digital Point-and-Shoot Cameras

In the right hands, digital point-and-shoot cameras can be used to create award-winning animations (like *Nightly News at Nine–Chapter 1*, which was made with a point-and-shoot camera).

- **Strengths:** High resolution, good picture quality, some have a manual mode for full control
- **Weaknesses:** Many are battery powered (make sure to research power adapters), and most cannot be easily connected to animation software
- **Recommended for:** Mid-level animators who value manual control and image quality and don't mind animating without the assistance of software
- **We suggest:** Canon PowerShot cameras (for example, SX60 and similar)

DSLR Cameras

DSLR (digital single-lens reflex) cameras are what professional animators and photographers use. They offer the most control over the look of your image; however, all this control comes at a price. DSLR cameras can cost thousands of dollars, and they have complicated controls that aren't intuitive to a novice photographer. You should definitely be committed to animation (and photography) before purchasing one of these cameras.

- **Strengths:** Highest resolution, best picture quality, can use many different lenses
- **Weaknesses:** Very expensive, complicated interfaces, not for beginners
- **Recommended for:** Advanced animators with deep pockets
- **We suggest:** Canon EOS cameras (for example, 7D Mark II or similar)

DSLR cameras are the way to go for pros.

Other Cameras

Any camera in the world can be used for stop-motion animation. Do you have an old film camera sitting in your basement? A tiny spy camera in your watch? A system of security cameras in your fallout shelter? With a little ingenuity, you could use any of these to make your next masterpiece. A great example of creative camera use is *A Boy and His Atom: The World's Smallest Movie*, whose creators filmed it on a microscope and animated it by manipulating individual atoms!

Once you select the camera you'll use to animate, you might have questions about how to use it to get the shots you want. Skip ahead to Chapter 8 if you're aching to learn more about cinematography.

I AM FREQUENTLY ASKED WHAT CAMERA I USE—ON YOUTUBE, AT LEGO CONVENTIONS, AT THE GROCERY STORE, EVERYWHERE. I WAS ASKED SO MANY TIMES THAT I DECIDED TO WRITE THIS BOOK. I USE A CANON 7D. THERE, YOU CAN CLOSE THE BOOK NOW.

I BOUGHT A *MICRO FOUR THIRDS (MFT)* CAMERA BECAUSE I READ THEY'RE BETTER FOR STOP-MOTION ANIMATORS THAN DSLRs. MFTs THEORETICALLY HAVE LONGER LIFESPANS THAN DSLRs. HOWEVER, MFTs ARE NOT FULLY SUPPORTED BY THE STOP-MOTION SOFTWARE I USE, SO I HAVE TO WORK HARDER TO USE BASIC FEATURES.

IN ALL SERIOUSNESS, THE CANON 7D IS A PRETTY ROBUST CAMERA, AND IT DOES THE JOB I NEED IT TO DO FOR BOTH STOP-MOTION AND LIVE-ACTION VIDEO SHOOTING. FOR THE MOST PART, I'LL USE A 17–55MM ZOOM LENS TO FRAME ALL OF OUR SHOTS—THOUGH SOMETIMES I'LL SWAP IT OUT FOR A 10MM FISH-EYE OR A 60MM MACRO LENS.

FOR INSTANCE, I HAD TO MOUNT A SECOND CAMERA ON TOP OF MY MAIN CAMERA IN ORDER TO USE ONION SKINNING. IF I COULD GO BACK IN TIME, I WOULD HAVE BOUGHT A CAMERA THAT WAS FULLY COMPATIBLE WITH MY SOFTWARE.

Tripods and Camera Mounts

Okay, you've got a camera. Now you need to point it at the LEGO bricks you plan to animate. You might be tempted to just pick up your camera and photograph everything by hand, but unless you have literal arms of steel, we don't recommend it.

Using a Tripod

As it turns out, three is the magic number of legs for creating a flat, stable support. That's why photographers and cinematographers around the world use *tripods* to hold their cameras. If your animation surface is on top of a desk, then a tripod is a good investment. And if you're interested in photography and videography outside of animation, obtaining a tripod is a must.

Most cameras have a threaded screw hole on the bottom where you can connect a tripod. If you're using a smartphone or webcam and want to use a tripod, you may need to purchase an additional camera mount to attach your camera.

- **Strengths:** Very flexible, can be adjusted to various heights and angles
- **Weaknesses:** Not good if you're animating on the floor
- **Recommended for:** Animators with large sets or high animating surfaces, budding photographers
- **We suggest:** The AmazonBasics Tripod is a good, inexpensive option

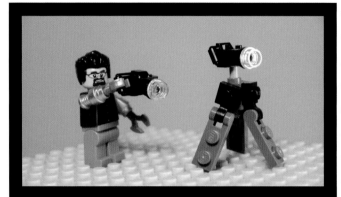

Tripods are a little easier to come by than cyborg arms...

...and they're great for getting a bird's-eye view of the action.

LEGO bricks and plates can raise your camera to the right height.

Using a Camera Mount

If you're filming on the floor or need to get an extreme close-up shot, a *camera mount* might do the trick. While there are products made specifically for close-to-surface filmmaking, most brickfilmers choose to build their own out of LEGO bricks.

- **Strengths:** Customizable, great for filming on the floor or other low surfaces
- **Weaknesses:** Not well suited for filming large-scale characters and sets

- **Recommended for:** Every brickfilmer will need a tabletop camera mount at some point
- **We suggest:** Build one by following the steps on the next few pages

In the spirit of LEGO building, we recommend that you design your own camera mount. This gives you ultimate creative control over the height, shape, and color of your mount.

Build a Camera Mount

1. Build a flat base out of plates that is at least 8 studs wider than your camera. Baseplates and large plates are great starting points for stationary mounts. Large plates make for a more versatile mount, but baseplates are easier to find.

2. Put one of your characters in front of the base as if you were about to animate. Hold your camera on or above the base so that the lens is eye level with the character. Can your camera stay in this position? If not, use some bricks to build a support structure. Take that, gravity!

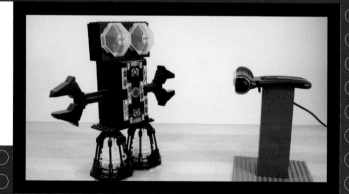

3. Now that you've got your camera at the right height, you need to make sure it doesn't wiggle from side to side or forward and backward. Build columns on all sides of your camera to lock it in place. Depending on the shape of the camera, you might need to use curved and angled pieces to get a snug fit. Remember to leave holes for accessing important buttons.

4. Is there room to safely build on the top of your camera? If so, build some connections between the columns with plates to firmly lock your camera in position.

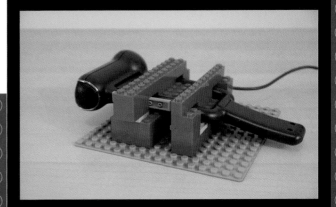

5. Planning some camera movement? Build some dolly rails out of tiles, and add some round pieces to the bottom of your mount so it can easily slide. Or go crazy with Technic pieces and build a gear-based crane or lift.

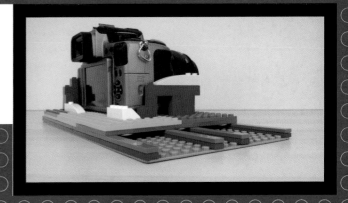

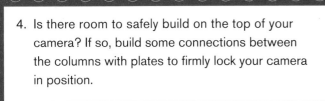

BRICK-BUILT CAMERA MOUNTS CAN BE HIGHLY VULNERABLE TO GRAVITY. MAKE SURE YOUR MOUNT IS STRONG AND SECURE SO THAT THE CAMERA DOESN'T TAKE A TUMBLE!

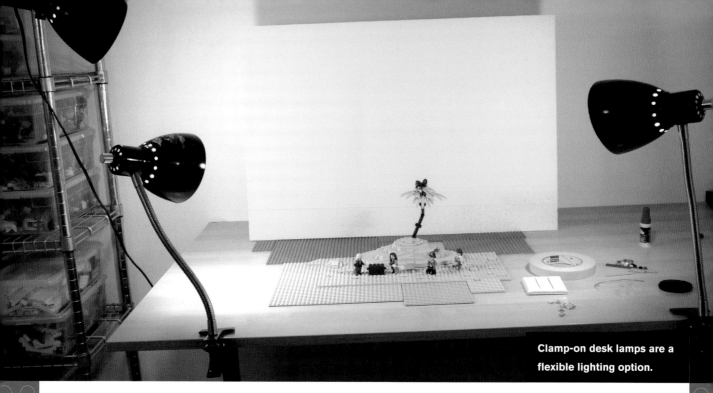

Clamp-on desk lamps are a flexible lighting option.

Lighting

Once you've got your camera of choice set up and ready to shoot, the next step is to light your animation set. There are two categories of lights used in brickfilms: big lights (aka human-scale lights) and tiny lights (aka minifig-scale lights).

Big Lights: Desk Lamps

One of the benefits of filming at minifigure scale is that desk lamps are big compared to the size of your characters and sets. A couple of regular lamps can provide all the light you need for animating a sunny day. If you already have some desk lamps, start with those. If you're buying new ones, we recommend getting clamp-on,

flexible-neck lamps and using daylight-balanced CFL bulbs. The blue-tinted light really brings out the colors of LEGO bricks, and CFLs provide a flicker-free light that will last a long time. LED bulbs are another perfectly viable option.

- **Strengths:** Inexpensive, easy to get new bulbs
- **Weaknesses:** Not easy to diffuse or color light, don't work for large-scale animations
- **Recommended for:** Brickfilmers working at minifigure scale
- **We suggest:** Clamp-on desk lamps with a flexible neck, daylight-balanced CFL bulbs

A pro lighting setup

Big Lights: Professional Light Kits

If you're dreaming big and want to work with giant sets or characters (think of brickfilms like *Little Guys!* or *Robota*), you might need more than just desk lamps. You'll probably need to put together a light kit like those used in live-action filmmaking. A basic brickfilming light kit includes the following:

- Three or more lights in a variety of sizes, with their power cords
- Extension cords and/or power strips
- At least one spare bulb per light
- Heat-resistant work gloves (for handling hot lights)

You can also purchase a basic, preassembled light kit. You have a wide range of options—from simple and inexpensive CowboyStudio kits to the pricey, sophisticated lights from companies like Lowel and Arri. We'll talk more about lighting tools in Chapter 8.

- **Strengths:** Provide a lot more light, have accessories for shaping and adjusting light
- **Weaknesses:** More expensive, take up a lot of space, require more electricity, not for beginners
- **Recommended for:** Animators with large sets and characters, animators who are also interested in producing live-action films, lighting geeks
- **We suggest:** Assemble your own kit, piece by piece

This treasure chest was lit from behind using LEGO Power Functions lighting.

Tiny Lights: LEGO Products

Sometimes you'll want to light only one part of your set—like a dark alley with a single street lamp, a spaceship with flashing lights, or a flickering torch in a cave. Tiny lights are great for providing this kind of environmental lighting.

The most recent official LEGO lighting element is the *Power Functions (PF)* light. PF lights are made to work within the LEGO system—the bulbs are the same diameter as a stud, and you can connect them to any tube or Technic pinhole. Don't forget to pick up a PF battery box and power adapter, as well as PF extension cables (if your lights need to be far away from the battery box). One limitation of PF lights is that the wires are relatively big, so they can be hard to hide from the camera.

You can also add light to your films by using glow-in-the-dark or transparent neon LEGO pieces. While they aren't lights themselves, these elements will glow under UV black lights. *Ghost Train* by Watercooler Productions is a good example of this approach.

- **Strengths:** Part of the LEGO system
- **Weaknesses:** Wires can be hard to hide, limited bulb shapes and colors
- **Recommended for:** LEGO purists, Technic and MINDSTORMS builders
- **We suggest:** LEGO Power Functions lights, rechargeable battery box with power adapter, and extension cables

These aliens' glowing eyes are powered by LifeLites NanoLites.

Tiny Lights: Third-Party Products

If you want to light up something *really* tiny (like a 1 × 1 transparent plate), the official LEGO lighting products may be too bulky. Luckily, there are some great third-party products designed to work with LEGO pieces. LifeLites and Brickstuff are two companies that sell super-tiny lights—tinier and brighter than even the LEGO PF elements. If you want to expand the environmental lighting in your brickfilm, lights from these folks may be the way to go.

- **Strengths:** Tiny, bright, come in different colors
- **Weaknesses:** More difficult to acquire and set up than LEGO lights, often better suited for MOC displays than for animation
- **Recommended for:** Lighting experts
- **We suggest:** LifeLites eLite Jr. Kit is a great entry product

Odds and Ends

- **Masking tape:** Use this to attach your sets and camera mount to your animating surface.
- **Brick separators:** These classic LEGO tools are great for quickly altering your set.
- **LEGO ruler:** Animation is mathy. You'll often need to count how many studs your character is going to walk. You can build a ruler using a few bricks and some clear tape.
- **Clear pieces:** Clear pieces are perfect for positioning a character or object slightly above the ground.
- **1×1 round plates:** Use these small pieces to keep track of characters and elements during animation.
- **Shooting tray:** Store all these odds and ends in a tray with customizable compartments to prevent a clutter-tastrophe.

- **Clamps:** We recommend clamps with rubber pads to prevent damaging your bricks.
- **Toothpick/straightened paper clip:** These are useful for moving minifig hands.

- **Glue:** Some see gluing bricks as a crime reserved for LEGO villains, but it's a technique many animators rely on.
- **Adhesive putty/sticky tack:** Putty is perfect for holding something in place temporarily.
- **Tiles and thin slopes:** Stick low-angle slope pieces under your characters or camera to tilt them just a little bit.
- **White balance piece:** We recommend a white 1×1×5 brick. It's about the size of a minifig, so it's easy to position in the same place as your characters.
- **Offset plates, turntables, hinges, joints, etc.:** These pieces are perfect for when a character needs to spin or lean.
- **Air balloon and brush:** Filming LEGO bricks in high definition makes every piece of dust seem enormous. Use an air balloon or brush to clean your set so dust doesn't steal the spotlight.

Microphones

You'll need a microphone if you plan to record dialogue or sounds for your animation. Budget-conscious filmmakers can get away with the built-in microphones on their computers or smartphones, but if you want the best sound quality, you'll need to upgrade to a stand-alone mic. Microphones range from simple models made for teleconferencing to high-end options for professional sound recording. The Blue Yeti and Snowball USB microphones are great if you can afford them, but most brickfilmers will be fine with a less expensive microphone.

Use a microphone for high-quality sound recording.

Computers

Computers can fill many roles in the production process—you can run animation software, listen to music while you're animating, pull up reference clips on YouTube, and edit your movie together. Beginning animators often rely solely on a smartphone or tablet, but experts usually graduate to a laptop or desktop computer. Here are some key specs to consider:

- **Compatibility:** Is the computer compatible with your camera, software, and other peripherals?
- **Processor speed and memory:** Editing and rendering video requires a lot of processor speed and memory. Having a fast processor (2 GHz or higher) and plenty of RAM (8GB or more) will speed up post-production significantly.
- **Portability:** If you plan to use your computer while animating, you'll need to have it close to your camera. A laptop computer might be more convenient, especially if you plan to animate in multiple locations.
- **Screen size:** If you're working with high-definition video, you'll want to be able to scrutinize the smallest details of your photos. A larger screen will make this easier.

We recommend the Apple MacBook Pro or a Dell Inspiron 7000 Series laptop or similar.

Software and Hardware Compatibility

Your camera, software, and computer, smartphone, or tablet must all be compatible—they need to be able to work together so that you can use them to make a film. If your software works on a Mac but your computer is a PC, you're out of luck. If your camera has an HDMI output but your computer takes only USB input, that won't work either. Even if your software is compatible with your computer and your camera is compatible with your computer, the camera might be unsupported by the software. It sounds crazy, but it happens.

That's why it's very important to check the compatibility of any animation software package, camera, or computer you're planning to buy before spending money.

Like two ill-fated lovers, this computer and smartphone can't seem to connect.

Compatibility Checklist

- **Buying animation software?** First, check the software product details to make sure it will run on your computer's operating system. Then, check the list of supported cameras to make sure it will work with yours.
- **Buying a camera?** First, check that its output cable has a matching input port on your computer. Then, check that the camera is supported by any animation software you're using.
- **Buying a computer?** First, check that it has an input port that matches your camera's output cable. Then, make sure any animation software you want to use will run on the computer's operating system.

Onion skinning helps you plan your movements carefully.

Stop-Motion Software

There's a stop-motion program out there for every type of animator, though the sheer number of options can be overwhelming. Here are some features to look for in your stop-motion software:

- **Onion skinning:** This overlays a transparent version of your last captured frame on top of your camera's live view. It's an invaluable feature for seeing how far you've moved your characters between frames. Onion skinning is also very helpful for getting your characters back in position if you accidentally knock them over.
- **Live playback:** Instant playback is essential for getting the timing of your character's actions just right. It's also cool to watch.
- **Camera support:** Make sure the software you choose can connect to your camera.

- **Remote capture:** The best stop-motion software will allow you to take pictures without touching your camera. This is great for avoiding set bumps.
- **Export options:** Some programs give you access to the raw photo files for each frame, while others only let you export a video file. Make sure the export options suit your post-production needs.
- **X-sheet:** Exposure sheets are great for keeping track of actions, dialogue, and more as you animate. Having these built into your software makes them even more useful.
- **Advanced features:** These include shooting on twos, multiple exposures, motion control, and more. (If you don't know what these advanced features are, then you probably don't need them.)

NOTE *Other useful software is covered in Chapter 9.*

Mobile Apps

Mobile apps are a great entry point for new animators—they're already connected to a camera and focus on the most basic functions. Searching an app store for "stop-motion" will reveal a number of options, many for free or only a few dollars. Stop Motion Studio by Cateater is a great free option that has all the basics. Stop Motion Studio Pro by Cateater and iStopMotion for iPad by Boinx Software are slightly more advanced (they allow more manual control of the camera, remote capture using two synced mobile devices, and more).

- **Strengths:** Easy to use, integrated with a camera, inexpensive
- **Weaknesses:** Lack advanced features, limited export options and storage space
- **Recommended for:** Beginners
- **We suggest:** Stop Motion Studio by Cateater (iOS, Android, Kindle, and Windows), iStopMotion for iPad by Boinx (iOS)

Mobile apps are an easy way to get started with stop-motion.

ANOTHER VALID OPTION IS TO SIMPLY *NOT* USE ANIMATION SOFTWARE—JUST MOVE YOUR CHARACTERS AND SHOOT THE PICTURES WITH YOUR CAMERA. "ANIMATING BLIND" MAY TAKE MORE GUESSWORK, BUT IT CAN BE JUST AS FUN AND REWARDING.

Desktop Software

Desktop software for stop-motion runs the gamut from fan-made homebrew products to official releases by established software companies. Some brickfilmers swear by free programs like Monkey Jam, Helium Frog, and StopMojo. Others prefer the stability and support of paid options like Stop Motion Pro and Boinx iStopMotion. Certain software packages have multiple tiers with different features, so make sure you're buying the one you need.

Pretty much all stop-motion software will have the same basic features, but camera support varies wildly from program to program. As always, be sure to do your homework.

- **Strengths:** Lots of features, can support webcams
- **Weaknesses:** Camera compatibility can be limited, homebrew options can be buggy
- **Recommended for:** Mid-level animators
- **We suggest:** Stop Motion Pro (PC), Boinx iStopMotion (Mac)

Desktop software offers more features.

Desktop Software: Dragonframe

Dragonframe is the be-all and end-all of stop-motion software. It's been used by professional studios to make big-budget movies like *Paranorman*, *Frankenweenie*, and *Shaun the Sheep*. It integrates pre-production tools like x-sheets, has a ton of features, and supports the most cameras—but it also costs the most.

We used Dragonframe to animate *The Magic Picnic*. We love it, but most brickfilmers will be fine using less complex software.

- **Strengths:** Has every feature you could possibly want, supports many cameras, comes with a special keypad for quickly accessing key features while animating
- **Weaknesses:** Overwhelming for beginners, expensive
- **Recommended for:** Advanced animators using DSLR cameras

Dragonframe: professional stop-motion software

Your Animation Toolkit

You might be itching to go out and buy a whole bunch of new supplies and accessories. That's great! Adding to your filmmaking toolkit is always fun. However, don't buy more equipment than you need, and make sure anything you buy complements, not complicates, your existing setup. Some of the world's greatest films (brick or otherwise) were made with simple tools. You should always put more care into what's on camera than what camera it's on.

Any of these animation setups can work just fine, as long as they are within your means and let you make the things you want to make.

7 The Creative Process

So far, we've talked a lot about the craft of LEGO animation, covering practical topics like how to organize your studio, design functional sets, animate characters, and so on. Now, let's explore the art of filmmaking—creating motion pictures to share your ideas and stories with other people.

Developing the idea for your film can be just as exciting and challenging as actually producing it. Over the course of our filmmaking and teaching careers, we've simplified film development into two main techniques: the Play Approach and the Plan Approach. These techniques will help you turn your basic ideas into completed movies. But first: how do you even come up with a film idea?

Brainstorming

People often ask us, "David(s), where do you get such crazy and awesome ideas for your LEGO animations?" Despite numerous brain scans, the alien scientists have yet to discover the ultimate source of our creativity—though they have noticed some recurring patterns. Here's a brief list of prompts for fruitful brainstorming, based on years of painful research.

- **Immerse yourself in the things you like.** What are your hobbies? What do you do for fun? Maybe you like camping, maybe you're in a band, or maybe you make decorative soaps. Whatever you enjoy, go do it, and consider the kinds of stories you can tell about it.

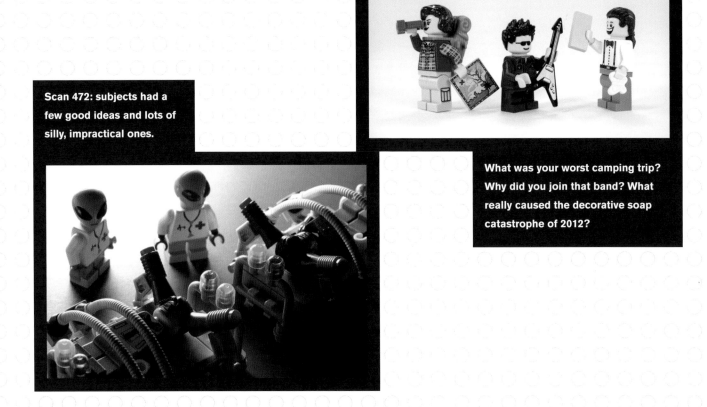

Scan 472: subjects had a few good ideas and lots of silly, impractical ones.

What was your worst camping trip? Why did you join that band? What really caused the decorative soap catastrophe of 2012?

Brainstorm while you work. (Whistling optional.)

- **Seek and embrace constraints.** Sometimes the best way to whip your creative brain into action is by setting limits for yourself. Film contests often have rules about the run time, theme, and style of entries. When starting a new project, try choosing an upcoming contest and using its deadline as a due date for your film. The race to finish in time while staying within contest guidelines can spark new and unexpected ideas.

- **Take a break from your film and do other things.** Clean your room, take a shower, run errands, or just leave your house. Taking a break from filmmaking can lessen the burden of coming up with an idea and will allow your mind to wander.

- **Remix other people's ideas.** Remixing preexisting ideas and stories is at the core of all works of art (even Shakespeare did it), so don't be afraid to

borrow things from other artists. Don't plagiarize, though—put your own spin on borrowed ideas, and give credit where credit is due.

- **Keep an idea journal on hand.** Ideas are sneaky creatures, so it's important to write them down before they slip away. You might be walking down the street and find yourself inspired by an interesting piece of trash, or you might wake from a dream with an idea for an elaborate musical number. Even if you can't use an idea for your current project, write it down—you never know when it might come in handy.

- **Brainstorm with LEGO bricks.** This is *The LEGO Animation Book*, after all, and we'd be remiss if we didn't talk about the creative potential in a pile of bricks. When in doubt, start building and see what happens.

WHEN I SET OUT TO MAKE *LITTLE GUYS!* I IMMERSED MYSELF IN ONE OF MY FAVORITE THINGS—RETRO TV ADS. I FOUND A FOUR-HOUR VHS TAPE OF 1980s COMMERCIALS ON EBAY AND WATCHED IT REPEATEDLY, TAKING NOTES ON RECURRING THEMES AND THE WAYS PEOPLE TALKED, AND MAKING SKETCHES OF THE TYPES OF CHARACTERS THAT SHOWED UP.

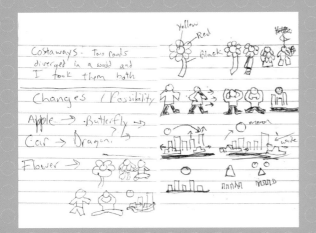

I OFTEN RELY ON CONTESTS AS THE CREATIVE FUEL FOR MY BRICKFILMS. MY FILM *METAMORPHOSIS* WAS INSPIRED BY THE 2010 BRICKS IN MOTION AVANT-GARDE CONTEST, BUT IT WAS THE MOFILM CANNES 2010 DEADLINE THAT MOTIVATED ME TO FINISH.

Ask Yourself "What If?"

Practically every film concept can be posed as a "what if?" question. This format is a great way to phrase your big ideas. See if you can recognize the films based solely on the following "what if?" questions:

- What if some explorers discovered a giant ape and brought it to New York City?
- What if some scientists discovered a way to capture ghosts and turned that into a business?
- What if a mermaid fell in love with a human?
- What if your toys came to life when you left the room?
- What if you fell in love with someone after hearing them on a radio call-in show?
- What if there was a machine that let you erase your bad memories?
- What if you could see what the world would be like if you had never been born?
- What if a man pretended to be a woman in order to get an acting job?
- What if a woman pretended to be a man in order to join the soccer team?
- What if a woman pretended to be a man pretending to be a woman in order to get a singing job?

Try turning your movie idea into a "what if?" question. Congratulations! You now have a movie pitch. You can use this basic question as a springboard to further develop the characters, plot, and other details of your film.

The Play Approach

Now that you've generated some ideas using our fool-proof brainstorming techniques, it's time to take those ideas and expand on them. The *Play Approach* is exactly what it sounds like: playing with your idea and letting your film emerge naturally.

How do you "play with an idea"? You can start with any of your LEGO creations. Place them in front of your camera and try making up a story one shot at a time. If you built a castle with a drawbridge, you could start with a shot of the drawbridge being lowered. Ask yourself "Why is the drawbridge coming down? Who is crossing it? Are they going into the castle or coming out of it?"

Keep going until you feel like the story is over, or you've shown off all the cool parts of your creation, or both.

You can also keep asking yourself questions about your story. For *The Magic Picnic*, we started with this "what if?" question: "What if two friends found a magic wand in the park?" From there, we asked more questions to develop the story:

- Who are Matt and Anna? What's their friend-ship like?
- What are they doing in the park?
- Where did they find the magic wand?
- What exactly does the wand do? How does it work?
- What if someone else got their hands on the wand?

Matt and Anna find a magic wand. What happens next?

Finding a story through the Play Approach can be as simple as goofing around with some minifigs.

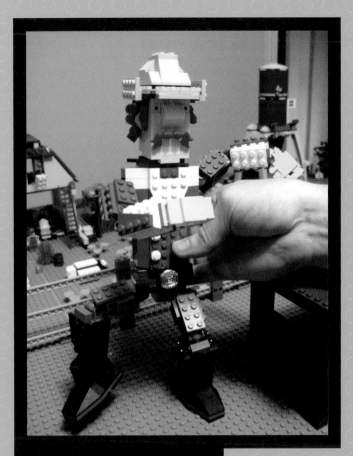

Play around with your characters to get an idea of how they might move or behave.

YOU CAN EVEN USE THE PLAY APPROACH TO MAKE FEATURE-LENGTH FILMS. TWO OF MY EARLIEST BRICKFILMS WERE 45- AND 60-MINUTE ANIMATIONS WHERE MY FRIENDS AND I MADE UP EVERYTHING AS WE WENT ALONG.

THEY WERE FULL OF TANGENTS, NON SEQUITURS, AND NONSENSE, BUT WE HAD A TON OF FUN MAKING THEM. THE PLAY APPROACH IS A GREAT WAY TO TRY IDEAS OUT.

One drawback of the Play Approach is that you might occasionally animate a scene or two that just doesn't fit into the story you end up telling. Cutting things out of any film can be a painful process. But if there are shots that don't add anything to (or worse, detract from) the story you want to tell, you've got to cut them out.

This reminds us of another "what if?" question: "What if there were a way to make sure that all of your shots show up in the final film?" Well, that's where the aptly named Plan Approach comes into, er, play.

The Plan Approach

The *Plan Approach* mimics the way big-budget feature films are made, and it goes something like this:

1. Brainstorm your idea.
2. Write a script.
3. Break the script up into a shot list.
4. Create storyboards.
5. Record the dialogue (if there is any) or song (if it's a music video).
6. Edit your storyboards into an animatic.
7. Design the necessary sets, characters, and so on.
8. Light and animate each shot of your film.
9. Replace the storyboards in the animatic with each completed shot.
10. Once all animatic shots have been replaced with final animation, add sound effects, music, and any other post-production effects.
11. Save and share your film!

By planning everything beforehand, you can be (relatively) sure that each frame you animate makes it into the final film. Just like with the Play Approach, your film is still going to change and evolve as you work on it. Your final product won't exactly match your storyboards or script; you'll simply use those as a guide to making the film.

Let's take a closer look at a few steps of the Plan Approach.

Writing a Script

With the Plan Approach, you'll expand your movie pitch into a full *script* (also known as a *screenplay*). The script is where you'll flesh out all of the action, set direction, and dialogue of your film in writing.

Script writing itself can also be broken down into "play" and "plan" approaches. You can outline the structure of the story and then write the script based on that, or you can take the seed of an idea and just start writing in a stream-of-consciousness style, and then see what grows out of it.

Script Formatting

In general, scripts contain a few basic elements:

- **Location:** Where is the action taking place? This is generally denoted as a broad description of the setting as an interior (INT) or exterior (EXT) location, followed by a more specific location and/or the time of day. Examples: "INT. DIMLY LIT LIVING ROOM—NIGHT" or "EXT. GRASSY PARK HILLSIDE—DAY."
- **Stage direction:** Describe what's happening in the scene. What are the characters doing? What's happening around them? Make sure your script tells the whole story. Examples: "Matt enters from off-screen left" or "Anna picks up the wand and studies it for a moment, then waves it around."

- **Dialogue:** Who's saying what? This is usually denoted by the character's name, followed by what they're saying. Example: "OLD WOMAN: Let me tell you a story about Anna and Matt…"
- **Camera and editing direction:** Your script could include ideas for camera placement and shot techniques. Examples: "DISSOLVE TO:" or "Camera pans to the left."

One thing to keep in mind when writing dialogue is that there's a difference between how people write and how people talk. When you're writing something down, you can take your time with word choice and grammar. When it comes to speaking, the words just flow directly from your mouth. Reading your dialogue aloud as you write it is the easiest way to make sure it sounds like something someone would actually say.

Depending on how much dialogue you have, you might want to do a *table read*. This is where all of the voice actors sit down at (what else?) a table, and read through the whole script from start to finish. It's another great way to get a feel for how the film flows, and to pick up on any dialogue or story areas that aren't working.

During your table read, you may find that certain sections of the script feel redundant or unnecessary. Cut them out! The whole point of screenwriting is to refine the story before you spend hours and hours animating. Good scripts need to go through multiple drafts to become great scripts (yes, your English teacher was right). Taking the time to refine your script will ultimately make your film stronger.

```
                    ROBOPHELIA
        I am Report-O-Bot Ophelia. I come
        to question you on behalf of the
        Figurians.

                    GRABBOR
        You are allied with the
        fleshblocks? Are you not a robot?

                    ROBOPHELIA
        I was built to protect, not invade.

                    GRABBOR
        Then you were built wrong.

                    ROBOPHELIA
        I have one last question: Are you
        ready to be destroyed?

        A fight ensues. ROBOPHELIA defeats GRABBOR.

                    GRABBOR
            (with dying battery) You- do not-
        compute.

        ROBOPHELIA takes GRABBOR's arm and attaches it to her body.
        She turns to the camera triumphant.

                    ROBOPHELIA
        Well, I think we settled that
        question. Back to you Phil!
```

Depending on the type of animation you're making, your script might include more stage direction and less dialogue, or vice versa. Compare these excerpts from the scripts of *NNN Chapter 2 – Robots!* and *The Magic Picnic*. Which one has more stage direction? Why?

```
        FADE IN:

        INT. LIVING ROOM - NIGHT

        An old woman stands next to a fireplace, holding an old
        book. She opens it, with the pages facing towards camera.

                    OLD WOMAN
            Let me tell you a story about Anna and Matt...

        The camera pushes in on the books pages, and we--

                                    DISSOLVE TO:


        EXT. GRASSY PARK HILLSIDE - DAY

        Two friends, ANNA and MATT, sit and share a picnic lunch. As
        they eat, a MAGIC WAND falls from the sky and lands between
        them.

        Matt picks up the wand, confused. He tries shaking the wand
        to activate it, but nothing happens. Matt LEGO-shrugs, and
        hands the wand to Anna, who begins examining it.

        With a flourish, Anna waves the wand towards the picnic
        basket... and it comes to life! The picnic basket starts
        moving around the blanket like a puppy.
```

You can write your script using a word processor like Microsoft Word or Google Docs.

Shot List

A *shot* is the basic unit of visual storytelling in film-making. From the time an image appears onscreen until the first cut to a new perspective—that's one shot. When the footage cuts to a new image, a new shot begins.

Once you're happy with your script, the next step is to create a shot list. This is where you'll break up your story into individual camera shots. Think about what you want to show on camera during each shot, and then write down a brief description of that mental image. Be sure to indicate what type of shot it will be (flip ahead to Chapter 8 to learn more about shot types).

A shot list comes in handy if you decide to shoot your film out of order. Thanks to the magic of editing, you can animate your shots in any order you like, and then rearrange them later into the correct sequence. There are a couple of reasons you might choose to shoot this way:

- If your film flips back and forth between a couple of different sets—for example, inside and outside of a house—you may want to animate all of the inside shots at once, and then animate all of the outside shots. This will save precious time and effort.

- By the time you finish your film, you'll be a much better animator than you were when you started. We recommend animating the middle shots first—that way, your best work can hit the audience at the beginning of the film, and stay with them at the end.

- Cool sets can take a long time to design, and you might get burned out on building every so often. Not a problem! Animate the shots you do have sets for, and then go back to building later.

SHOT LIST

INT Living room (Area 1)

1. WS old woman (minifig size with digital mouth), holding a book. She says "Let me tell you a story about Anna and Matt..." She opens it as we slow zoom in on the book and FADE TO

EXT Microscale City (Area 6)

2. EWS microscale city indistinct in bg. FADE TO:

EXT Town - picnic area (Area 2)

3. WS Picnic area, where ANNA and MATT sit on a blanket. As they eat lunch, a wand falls from the sky and lands in between them.
4. CU Wand on picnic blanket.
5. MS Matt is confused by the wand. Shake, nothing happens, offers it to anna offscreen left. Pan left to Anna, who accepts the wand and examines it.
6. WS hillside, same as 3. Anna uses the wand to make the picnic basket move. Anna ends her wand usage, and offers it back to matt, who is excited.
7. MS Matt, who looks at the wand, determined. He points it down towards screen left to zap the basket.
8. CU basket, a zap comes in from screen right, and transforms the basket into silly object #1.
9. MCU Anna reacts, amused.
10. CU basket, same as 8. More zaps come in and rapidly transform apple into silly objects #2-10. Object #10 is a robot, who starts walking around.

Part of the shot list for *The Magic Picnic*

Storyboarding

Once you're happy with your shot list, it's time to move on to the storyboarding phase. *Storyboarding* is the use of drawings to illustrate and sketch out your film.

There are many ways to approach storyboarding. Some folks draw each shot of the film as one panel (like a comic strip); others go further and flesh out the movement and acting poses. It all depends on what your film is about, and where it will end up being seen. Here are some scenarios to consider:

- Is it a character study? Then you might want to use your boards to plan out the character's performance in detail.
- Is it an action movie? Then you'll probably end up using the boards to figure out how the characters move, and where they are in relation to one another in space.
- Are you making a commercial? Storyboards can be useful to make sure you've got all the necessary product beauty shots.
- Do your storyboards need to be approved by someone else by a certain deadline? Then you'll want to make sure that the boards are as clear and concise as possible.

Here's a sample storyboard to get you started. You can find a template for this storyboard on the book's website at *https://www.nostarch.com/legoanimation/*. Most modern brickfilms are shot in a 16:9 widescreen ratio, but we've also included a 4:3 guideline overlay for retro full-screen fun. (Refer to Chapter 8 for more on aspect ratios.) The template also includes space for a shot number and description.

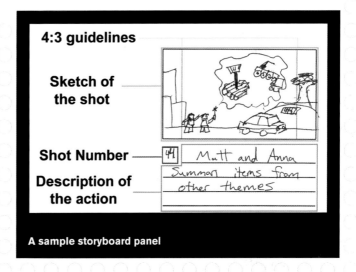

Storyboards don't need to be detailed or complex. They just need to tell you what happens in the scene.

4:3 guidelines

Sketch of the shot

Shot Number

Description of the action

A sample storyboard panel

Now that you've got a feel for how storyboards are laid out, let's look at a sequence of boards from *The Magic Picnic*. We've included screenshots from the final animation for comparison—notice how they don't always match the storyboards exactly.

03 A wand falls onto Anna and Matt's picnic blanket

04 CU wand on blanket

Exercise: Storyboard a Scene from Your Favorite Movie

Artists hone their technique by copying from the masters. Select a scene from one of your favorite movies and, with your hand resting near the pause button, scroll through the scene and sketch the various shots. Your sketches don't have to be perfect; they just need to have enough information to convey what's going on in the shot.

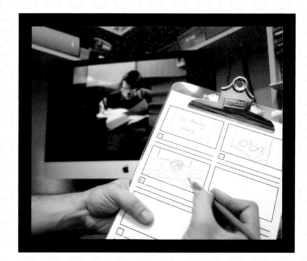

05 | Matt is confused by the wand

Animatics

Once you've created your storyboards, it's time to edit them together into an *animatic* (also called a *story reel*). Put each of your shots in sequence using editing software (see Chapter 9) and keep each storyboard onscreen for about as long as you want the shot to appear in the final film. This will help you get a feel for how long each shot will last and how the sequence will flow. You might find that you need to change the timing, add some more drawings, or take some away. This is totally normal—boarding and reboarding is a natural part of sculpting your film. The earlier you can identify and address the issues in your film, the better.

Even though we won't be talking about sound design until Chapter 9, the animatic phase is also the time where you might place some rough sound into your film. You don't need to go too crazy with sound effects, but some temporary music tracks or rough dialogue (usually recorded by the animator, replaced by the voice actors' recording later) can be helpful in constructing your film.

You can watch the animatic for *The Magic Picnic* at https://www.nostarch.com/legoanimation/.

DRAWING HAS NEVER COME NATURALLY FOR ME, SO I SOMETIMES CREATE WHAT I CALL A "PHOTO ANIMATIC." RATHER THAN USING STORYBOARDS, I TAKE STILL PHOTOS OF EACH SHOT AND CUT THOSE TOGETHER INSTEAD.

PICK THE TYPE OF ANIMATIC THAT WORKS BEST FOR YOU. YOUR AUDIENCE WON'T SEE IT EITHER WAY—UNLESS YOU'RE PUTTING TOGETHER SOME BEHIND-THE-SCENES VIDEOS (OR WRITING A BOOK ABOUT LEGO ANIMATION).

DRAWING IS FUN!

Organizing Your Work with Spreadsheets

While you're in your planning bonanza, you can use those magic documents known as *spreadsheets* to keep track of your work.

We recommend using a program like Numbers, Excel, or Google Sheets to keep a detailed log of your shot list, including information like the shot number, how many frames long it is, camera specs, and so on. When all of your information is in a spreadsheet, you'll know where to look when starting the next shot.

You can also use a spreadsheet to plot out the frame-by-frame actions of each individual shot in your film. These types of spreadsheets are commonly known as *exposure sheets* or *X-sheets*. They have rows for each frame of a given shot, and columns you can customize for details like lip sync, camera positions, or anything else you might want to keep track of while animating.

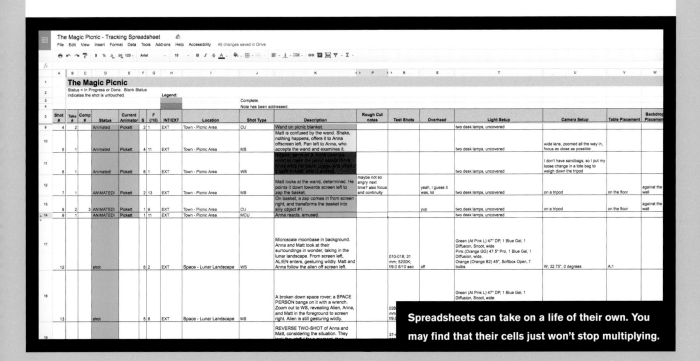

Spreadsheets can take on a life of their own. You may find that their cells just won't stop multiplying.

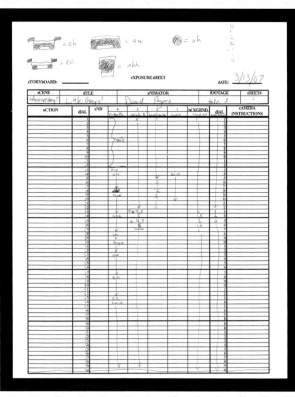

You can make fancy exposure sheets using a computer, or you can draw them by hand while riding public transportation so strangers think you're a crazy person. (Or you can download a template from our book's website at *https://www.nostarch.com/legoanimation/*.)

Filmmaking is a juggling act. Keeping too many balls in the air while hunched over your animation surface is a tall order, even for the most seasoned performers. Use these methods to map it all out, and then fire up your camera and animate something really sweet.

Plan out the technical aspects of your film. Then you can float through animation with the greatest of ease.

Cinematography
and Production

8

So far, we've talked about how to make your sets and characters look and move as best as they can. While building neat stuff for your film is certainly important, it's also important to think about how to capture those things in photographic form.

Everything we talked about in Chapter 7 technically falls under the banner of *pre-production*—conceiving the film, developing ideas for each shot, and preparing to shoot your film. This chapter will take you into the *production* process of filmmaking. This is where you'll set up and animate all of the shots for your brick-film masterpiece. We'll cover topics like frame rate, lighting, and focus to help you shoot a stunning film. We'll also introduce you to the art of *cinematography*, which is all about designing shots and taking great pictures.

Aspect Ratio

First things first: let's think about the shape of your frame, also known as the *aspect ratio*. The aspect ratio is the relationship between the width and the height of the image.

To decide which aspect ratio is right for you, think about where your film will be viewed. Do you imagine people watching your film on YouTube, in front of a television, or on their phone? No matter what kind of screen your film ends up on, you can find an aspect ratio to match.

When choosing an aspect ratio, there are a few things to bear in mind:

- **Aesthetics:** Your aspect ratio can help give your film a particular tone. Wide aspect ratios can convey a sense of epic scope, while narrow ones might feel more retro and personal.
- **Time period:** Aspect ratios can also sell the illusion of your film being created in a specific era. If you

want your film to look like a 1960s TV broadcast, 4:3 is the best choice—it was the aspect ratio for '60s television. Wes Anderson's film *The Grand Budapest Hotel* is a great example of this approach.
- **Camera limitations:** Check your camera to see which aspect ratios you can shoot. If your camera doesn't shoot the size you want, you can crop your animation to the correct size later on. We shot *The Magic Picnic* at 3:2 and then cropped it to 16:9.
- **Practicality:** If your characters and sets are all wildly different sizes, it may be easier to arrange them onscreen with certain aspect ratios. Shoot some test photos to make sure you can position everything the way you want.

If you're not sure which screen shape is right for you, 16:9 is a safe middle ground. This is the size of most televisions, YouTube videos, and theatrical films.

1:1 is a perfect square—the default aspect ratio of Instagram, Vine, and other social media outlets.

2.35:1 is one of many widescreen cinema standards. This is often what you see on the big screen!

4:3 is the aspect ratio for standard-definition (i.e., old) TV sets and computer monitors.

16:9 is the current standard aspect ratio for high-definition videos, televisions, games, and computer screens.

Frame Rate

Deciding on a frame rate before you begin animating will help your film look consistent. Higher frame rates like 30 FPS may mean smoother motion, but you'll have to take a lot more pictures. Lower frame rates can look choppy, but fewer pictures mean less work for you.

We recommend 12 or 15 FPS as a happy medium. Whether you pick a high or low frame rate, try to choose one that's a factor of 24 (6, 8, 12, or 24 FPS) or 30 (5, 6, 10, 15, or 30 FPS). This will be important when you export your film.

Regardless of what frame rate you choose, remember: *more frames do not equal better animation*. Taking additional pictures is not a magic cure-all; you can pick the highest frame rate possible and still come out with jittery animation. If you find yourself overwhelmed by taking pictures, try a lower frame rate! As long as you practice the principles of animation that we covered in Chapter 3, any frame rate you choose can give you a great result.

Waving a wand at 5 FPS

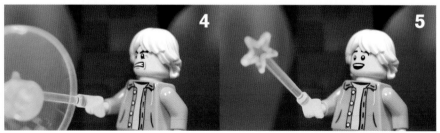

Opposite page: the same one-second-long clip at 15 FPS.

Take Your Shot

As we saw in Chapter 7, the shot is the basic unit of visual storytelling in filmmaking. No matter which approach you follow (Play or Plan), you'll need to make specific choices about how to set up each of your shots.

When you *frame* a shot, you decide where the camera will go and in which direction it will point. Most shots are characterized by two things: the *shot type*, which is how much of the scene is onscreen, and the *shot movement*, which is how the camera moves in relation to the scene.

Shot Types

Let's start with a few standard shot types.

A *very wide shot (VWS)* shows the subject of the scene and the environment in equal prominence.

A *wide shot (WS)* favors the subject as the focal point of the shot while still showing plenty of the surrounding area.

A *medium shot (MS)* focuses on the subject but doesn't necessarily show the whole thing.

A *close-up (CU)* moves in even tighter, focusing on one part of the subject in particular (in this case, the head).

An *extreme close-up (ECU)* is self-explanatory.

Shot Movement

Once you have an idea of what kind of shot you want to use, you can add movement to make it more dynamic.

Horizontal (x-axis) shot movement

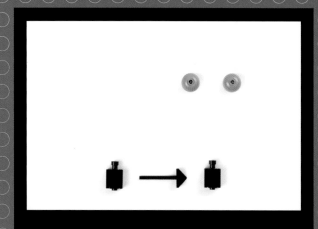

If the camera itself moves horizontally in space, it's called *tracking*.

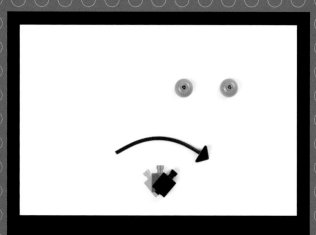

If the camera stays in one place but rotates, it's called a *pan*.

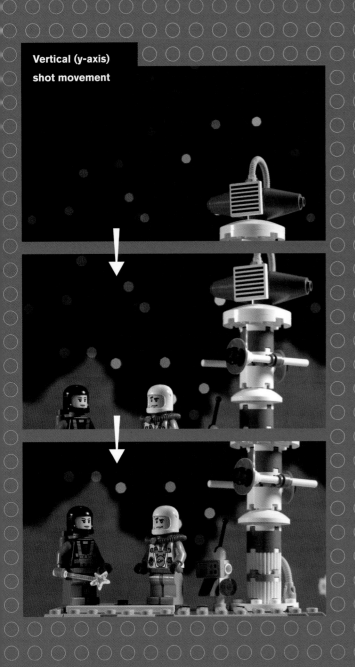

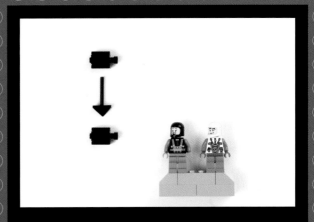

If the camera itself moves vertically in space, it's called a *pedestal*.

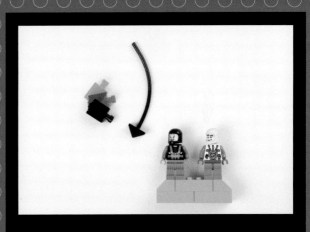

If the camera tilts up and down to accomplish the shot movement, it's called, well . . . a *tilt*.

Shot movement along the z-axis (depth)

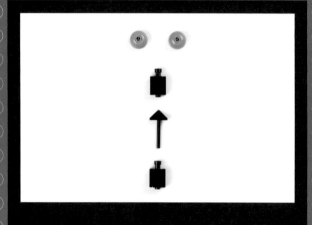

If the camera itself moves forward or backward, it's called a *dolly*. If the camera stays put but the lens pushes in on the subject (this movement happens inside the camera lens), it's called a *zoom*.

I LIKE TO DO MY SHOT MOVEMENT ON-SET— WHICH MEANS THAT I HAVE TO MOVE MY CHARACTERS *AND* THE CAMERA AT THE SAME TIME. I USE CRANKABLE TRIPODS FOR PEDESTAL MOVES, KITCHEN TURNTABLES FOR ROTATION, HOMEMADE DOLLY TRACKS, AND A *LOT* OF MATH TO FIGURE OUT THE TIMING AND SPACING.

DON'T BE AFRAID TO USE EVERY TRICK IN THE BOOK (LITERALLY—THIS BOOK) TO GET THE SHOTS YOU WANT!

Once you know these basic shot approaches, you can combine them for interesting results. For example, a shot can start out as a close-up on a character and then pan over to a wide shot of the surrounding area.

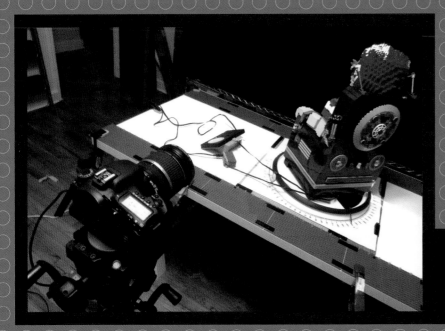

One shot from *Little Guys . . . In Space!* used a rotating kitchen tray on top of a sliding baseplate to add some movement to the scene.

This tripod already had wheels, so with a few bits of scrap wood . . . voilà! A DIY dolly track.

Shot Composition

The next step is to consider how you want to compose your shots. *Composition* is the art of arranging your characters, props, vehicles, sets, and anything else you want in the scene.

There are many ways to compose a shot, but here are a few basic guidelines. Once you're familiar with these rules, you can play with them to get different reactions from your audience.

- **The rule of thirds:** One way to create interesting compositions is to imagine the frame divided into thirds both horizontally and vertically. You can arrange your shot so that certain parts end up sitting along the dividing lines, at their intersections, or in between.

- **Headroom:** If your shot focuses on a character, you'll typically want to keep their head from being too close to or too far from the top of the screen. Try using the rule of thirds as a guide for where the character's eyes should go.

In this photo, Matt and the tree are sitting at an intersection point. The sky, the city background, and the grass each take up roughly one-third of the frame.

- **The 180 degree rule:** If you've got two characters talking to each other, it's important for the audience to know where they are in relation to each other. To follow the 180 degree rule, draw an imaginary line through your characters. For all of the shots in the sequence, keep the camera on one side of that imaginary line. This helps keep their spatial relationship clear.

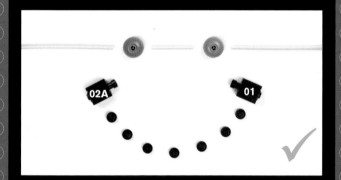

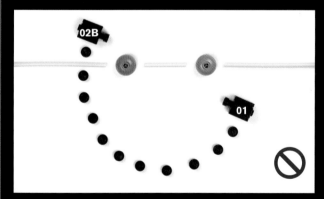

The corresponding shots. When you obey the 180 degree rule, two characters conversing remain on the same side of the screen between shots (01 and 02A). When the 180 degree rule is broken (01 and 02B), the characters appear to switch sides—confusing their locations.

The correct application of the 180 degree rule places the camera for shot 01 and 02A on the same side of the imaginary line. If the camera "jumps the line," your sequence of shots can become confusing.

- **Forced perspective:** If you can't fit everything you want onscreen at once, try using background elements that are built to a scale smaller than the main subject of your shot. This can add depth to the scene and allow you to achieve shot compositions that wouldn't otherwise be possible. (For more on working with different scales, flip back to Chapter 5.)

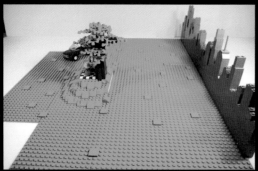

What looks like a sprawling city far off in the distance is really just a microscale skyline sitting less than 10 inches away.

Light 'Em Up

Turning a light on is easy—you just flip a switch. Using lights to mimic reality in your brickfilm takes a little more effort. Now we'll teach you more about the art of lighting and the various ways it can add texture and tone to your shots.

Let There Be Light Safety!

Lights are probably the most dangerous part of any stop-motion production. Working with electrical equipment can be dangerous, and lights can get hot to the point where you can burn yourself. If you need to readjust your lights between shots, turn them off and wait until they are cool. If you're putting colored gels or diffusers in front of a light, remember that they can melt or catch fire. If you plug too many lights into a single electrical outlet, it can short-circuit or blow a fuse. And, of course, if you look directly into a bright light, you can damage your eyes.

Be extra careful when working with anything electrical. Find someone experienced to help you set up and take down your lights.

The most basic approach to lighting a shot is called *three-point lighting*. This uses, unsurprisingly, three lights. Let's look at the three-point lighting system in action.

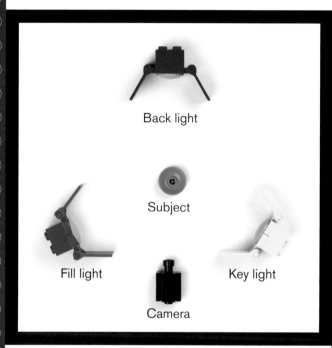

Back light

Subject

Fill light

Key light

Camera

- The green circle represents a character—in this case, it's Anna.
- The black camera-shaped object is the camera.
- The *key light* (in yellow) is the main light on the front of your subject (generally off to one side). This is typically the brightest of the three, and it sets the overall brightness of the scene.
- The *fill light* (in blue) fills in the shadows caused by the key light and balances out the lighting of the scene. Fill light is usually a bit dimmer than the key light so as to avoid flat lighting on your subject.

- The *back light* (in red, also known as a *hair light*) is usually overhead and behind the subject and helps to separate the subject from the background. Be careful when positioning your back light—if it points at the camera too directly, it can cause a lens flare.

The following series of photos shows each light in the three-point lighting system and how the lights combine to affect the overall lighting scheme of a shot.

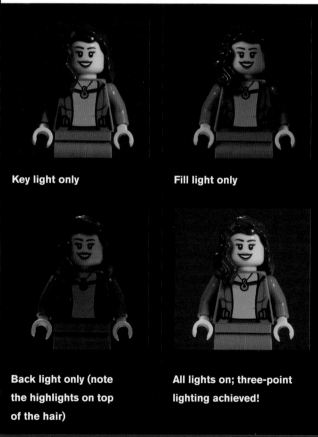

Key light only

Fill light only

Back light only (note the highlights on top of the hair)

All lights on; three-point lighting achieved!

Mood Lighting

The three-point lighting system is a great starting place for getting clear, bright shots, but sometimes you don't want a bright shot. For instance, if a scene is set in an alley or a dark room, you'll want to emphasize the shadows.

Adding colored light can also change the mood of a scene. Blue is often used for nighttime scenes, while red light can represent fire or simply add an eerie feeling to a film. To add color to your film, you can either use colored light bulbs or place a tinted sheet of plastic between your light and the scene. (Be sure to refer back to "Let There Be Light Safety!" on page 166.)

Red light is perfect for creepy campfire sing-alongs.

This shot under the bleachers uses a bright backlight to create shadows.

Hard and Soft Light

Because LEGO bricks and minifigures are made of super-shiny plastic, they reflect any light source very easily—even when you don't want them to. When using your average desk lamp, you may find that the light is too harsh, or too *hard*.

Hard light is the type of light you tend to get from bare bulbs. It casts intense shadows, creating a high contrast and strong glare. You'll often get hard light when using a light source that's smaller than the scene you're trying to light. Hard light definitely has its uses (like creating dramatic shadows), but it can make lighting for LEGO animation difficult.

To get even lighting and avoid unwanted glare, you can turn hard light into *soft light* by diffusing it.

Diffusion is the process of scattering light across a larger area—perfect for highly reflective LEGO sets and characters. You can diffuse the lights on your set in a couple of ways:

- Instead of pointing the light directly at the set, aim it at a white wall or board so it bounces off and lights your scene indirectly.
- Place some kind of material between the light and your set. You can use any semitransparent white fabric or paper for this. We recommend using baking parchment paper, as it's inexpensive and resistant to high temperature.

Diffusing the light on your set creates a soft, even look and reduces the amount of reflection and glare on your LEGO models.

Two common options for light diffusion: On the left is a *softbox*—a light inside a reflective box covered in translucent fabric. On the right is a light with a piece of diffusion paper pinned to the front.

Light Flicker

If you've completed the basic animation exercise in Chapter 1, you may have noticed a peculiar phenomenon: sometimes, for seemingly no reason, the lighting in your animation will appear to flicker during playback. This happens to everyone—even us!

While it seems like it happens for no reason, this inconstant lighting often happens for *too many* reasons. Flicker can be caused by any number of factors, like how your camera takes pictures, the types of bulbs you're using, what you're wearing, ambient light, or uneven flooring.

Here are some tips for avoiding flicker that have worked for us. Try a couple of different solutions to see which one works for your setup:

- Check that none of your camera's automatic settings are turned on.
- Avoid wearing bright clothing.
- Limit unnecessary movement around the room.
- Avoid animating on a rickety surface or carpeted floor.
- Point all ambient light sources (such as computer monitors or digital clocks) away from your set.
- Don't run power-draining appliances (for example, microwaves, dishwashers, washing machines) while animating.
- Stand back from the set, and stay in the same area of the room when taking each picture.

Taking a few test frames before you hunker down to animate can also help you determine which light flicker sources need to be addressed.

This removable sun-blocking window cover was made using a masonite board and inexpensive rails from a hardware store.

THERE IS ONE OTHER MAJOR CAUSE OF LIGHT FLICKER: *THE SUN*. THE SUN IS YOUR NEMESIS. IT'S IMPOSSIBLE TO CONTROL. IF YOU CAN'T SET UP YOUR STUDIO IN A WINDOWLESS ROOM, TRY BLOCKING THE SUNLIGHT WITH LARGE BOARDS OR BLACKOUT SHADES.

FOR AN EVEN CHEAPER SOLUTION, USE BLACK GARBAGE BAGS OR ALUMINUM FOIL. FOIL HAS THE ADDED BENEFIT OF PREVENTING ALIENS FROM READING YOUR MIND.

Motivated Lighting

Another way to make your lighting look even better is to plan motivated light sources. *Motivated lighting* is an approach that imitates where light would be coming from in the world of your film.

For example, if you're shooting a daytime scene in a character's living room, there could be lamps or over-head lighting in that room that would act as the light source. You could also set up a light outside the room, to approximate the sun.

But what if it's a nighttime scene? The sun is gone, but maybe now there's moonlight outside the window. If the characters are watching television, the TV screen might cast some light on them as well.

Matching the lighting scheme of your scene to the setting and mood you're trying to convey is essential to achieving a cinematic look.

Motivated lighting uses the real world for reference. What a bright idea!

Get into Focus

Focus up! It's time to animate the first shot of your film.

First you'll want to adjust the *focus*—this is where you'll select which parts of the shot are clear and which are blurry. Focusing tells your audience which things they should be paying attention to. Since brickfilms typically deal with small-scale characters and sets, it can be difficult to get everything into focus at once. In these situations, you'll need to get creative about which elements of the scene you want to keep sharp.

Many cameras have a setting for shooting tiny objects. *Macro focus mode* (which we briefly discussed in Chapter 6) is usually designated by either the word *macro* or a picture of a flower.

The macro focus setting on a point-and-shoot camera, denoted by the flower icon

In this sequence of photos, the focus moves from Anna (who is closest to the camera) to Matt (who is farther away) to the mountainside (way in the background). When one area is clear and sharp, the others become blurry.

Set the Exposure

If your camera allows for it, this is also the time to adjust exposure settings. These will affect the brightness, color, and clarity of your photos.

- The *aperture* setting determines the size of the hole that will open in the lens to let light into your camera, and it's measured in f-numbers (for example, f/5.6, f/8). The smaller the f-number, the wider the aperture will open, and the more light there will be.
- The *shutter speed* determines how long the aperture will remain open. This is typically measured in fractions of a second (for example, 1/8, 1/10) or in seconds for really long shutters.
- The *ISO* setting determines how sensitive the camera is to light. The higher the ISO number, the less light you need to take a picture—but at the cost of adding a lot of grain (fuzziness) to your images.
- The *white balance* setting allows you to select a white object in your scene that the camera will treat as white. That way, the colors of your set will match the colors in your images.

It can take years of practice to truly master these camera settings. For now, we recommend learning what each term means and eyeballing whether a shot looks the way you want. Again, taking some test photos prior to animation can help you make sure things look correct.

Set the white balance on your camera to make your colors stand out.

And . . . Action!

Like so many things in life, stop-motion is a marathon, not a sprint. Once you take that first picture, you're probably going to want to keep powering through until you finish animating the entire shot. (You just might have some fun, too.)

Check your progress as you go to make sure you're satisfied with how the shot looks. If you're using animation software, there will most likely be built-in tools to help make this easier. Be sure to take advantage of features like these:

- Standard *playback controls*, to review your progress
- *Onion skinning*, which lets you overlay the last picture you took onto the live feed as a semitransparent image

- Settings to *toggle* between frames or to *loop* the playback of your animation progress

There's really not much more to say about production at this point. Once your first shot is done, it's on to the second! And then the third, and the fourth, and the fifth . . .

If you're animating solo, just relax and take your time getting through the shot. If you've got a friend to animate with you, you can have them review the playback while you animate the characters; then, if they're game, switch roles on the next shot.

9 Post-production

By now, you've already put a lot of work into your LEGO animation masterpiece. You've scripted (or improvised) an interesting story, built cool characters and stable sets, and animated some fun, dynamic scenes. Your movie is almost complete—you just need to put it all together. In this chapter, we'll look at sound design, video editing, digital effects, and ways to share your film.

Post-production involves a lot of cutting and a little bit of magic.

Sound

So far, we've focused on the visual aspects of film-making, but that's only half of the puzzle. Sound is also an extremely important part of any film. It adds another dimension to your stories and gives your audience vital information—sometimes subconsciously. Sound has been a part of motion pictures almost from the very beginning; even the earliest "silent films" often had music.

If sound is so important, why did we put this section at the very end of the book? For most beginning animators, sound is the last element added to an animated film. If you're making your first animation or following the Play Approach from Chapter 7, you can safely forget about sound until the very end of the filmmaking process. But if you want your visuals to perfectly sync up with the audio (like in a music video), you'll want to plan ahead and finalize certain parts of the soundtrack before shooting a single frame.

Whether you're playing or planning, the basics of sound design are the same. There are three main types of sound and various ways to record or acquire them.

Types of Sound

- **Music:** Music can set the mood of a scene or help your audience understand how a character is feeling. Action sequences like car chases usually have fast-paced, high-energy music, while dramatic scenes might have slower or quieter music.
- **Sound effects:** The sounds made by vehicles, animals, machines, weather, explosions, and so on are considered sound effects. Sound effects can accentuate the actions happening onscreen or tell the audience about something happening off-screen. A well-timed sound effect can increase the impact of a character's action—a punch without the punch sound might not seem as real to the audience.
- **Dialogue:** When characters in a film speak (to themselves, to each other, or directly to the audience), it's called *dialogue*. Some films contain a lot of dialogue, and others don't have any.

Recording Sound

Whenever possible, we recommend recording your own sound. This gives you opportunities to be creative in a new medium, and it ensures that you own the rights to your entire film. You can use things around the house to create sound effects and ask your friends or family to help you do voices. But first things first: you'll need to set up a recording "booth."

Large closets make excellent recording booths.

While digital cameras make it easy to take great pictures almost by accident, it's hard to accidentally get good sound. That's why it's important to do some basic soundproofing so that you record only the sounds you want. Start by taking your microphone and computer to the quietest area you can find—for example, a carpeted bedroom, office, or closet—and then follow these tips to reduce unwanted sounds:

- Don't record in a noisy area—avoid loud computer fans, kitchen appliances, pets, and so on.
- Try putting a blanket at the base of the door to muffle unwanted sound from other rooms.
- To avoid echo, cover the walls with soft objects like blankets, pillows, or fabric curtains.
- Sit in a chair that doesn't squeak.
- When recording dialogue, use a pop filter to reduce unwanted mouth sounds.
- Keep your face a few inches away from the microphone (about 6 inches is optimal).

Now that you've set up a quiet recording booth, it's time to make some noise! You can record using a voice memo app on a smartphone or using desktop software like Audacity or Pro Tools.

Music

If you are musically talented (or have a friend who is), composing original music for your film will make it feel extra special. Composers can start thinking up musical ideas after seeing an animatic, but it's usually good to wait until the film is shot and edited to finalize a composition; this ensures that the music matches the action onscreen perfectly. Once the music is written, you can record it in your recording booth using real instruments or use a computer program like GarageBand to synthesize it.

Sound Effects

The process of creating sound effects is called *foley*. Rather than going out and recording the actual sound effect, foley artists re-create a similar sound using everyday objects. For instance, rather than putting their microphone next to a real bomb, a foley artist might re-create the sound of an explosion by dropping a heavy book on a table.

Try doing some foley with LEGO bricks. For the sound of rain, you could drop a lot of little round pieces on a table. For the sound of footsteps, try tapping a long brick against a big, flat baseplate. Feel free to mix in other household items like rubber bands, wooden blocks, or silverware to create other sounds.

Dialogue

If you're recording dialogue, start by trying to enter the emotional headspace of your character; what are they thinking and feeling when they say this line? Try recording the same line or sound effect several different ways; you can pick the best version later. And don't be afraid to go off-script; some of the most memorable lines in film history were improvised.

Search your collection for elements that can make interesting noises when tapped, scratched, or dropped, and use them to make your own sound effects.

Using Other People's Sounds

The internet has made it very easy to acquire all sorts of sounds. Practically any song or sound effect you can imagine can be found with a quick search. However, just because it's possible to download a sound file and import it into your editing program doesn't mean you have legal permission to use that sound in your film (even if you paid for it).

Without getting into murky legal territory (we're animators, not lawyers), a good rule of thumb is to avoid using sounds created by other people unless you have express written permission or you've paid for a royalty-free use. Many film contests will disqualify you for using audio you don't have the rights to use, and platforms like YouTube may take down films that contain copyrighted music.

Fortunately, there are many generous creators who make their sound effects and music available for anyone to use for free. We've listed a few of our favorite resources for free sounds on the book's website (*https://www.nostarch.com/legoanimation/*).

Editing

Editing is all about taking the raw materials that make up a film—pictures, sounds, and digital effects—and arranging them to create a seamless final product. If you're creating your first animation (with the approach we covered in Chapter 1), your film might not require much editing. But as your films become more complex, editing will become more important.

There are many steps to editing a film, but they can be done in pretty much any order. If you're following the Play Approach from Chapter 7, most of your editing will likely take place at the end of production, after you've completed all the stop-motion work. If the Plan Approach is more your speed, then the majority of your film's editing will happen before you start animating, in the storyboard and animatic phases.

No matter which path you take, keep in mind that editing is a constant process throughout the making of your film; you'll always be cutting out what doesn't work and adding in what does. Here's our suggested approach for editors in training.

Step 1: Get Familiar with Your Software

As mentioned in Chapter 6, we recommend starting with the simplest and cheapest editing software to learn the basics (iMovie and Windows Movie Maker are great for beginners; Final Cut X and Adobe Premiere Pro are better for experts). Once you've picked a program, you'll need to spend some time getting to know how it works. Some programs have unique features, but most have the basics in common:

- **Library:** This is a window with a list of the content you've imported (video, sound, and still pictures). The library might also be labeled something like *project*, *media*, or *footage bin*. Depending on the program, your library may appear as a text list or a visual collage. You can drag clips from here into the timeline to add them to your movie.
- **Timeline:** This is where your movie comes together. The timeline is a visual representation of all the clips you've added to the movie, laid out in the order in which they'll play back. Some programs call the timeline a *sequence* because the clips are in sequential order. Rearrange clips in the timeline to change the order in which things happen in your movie. Video and audio clips are often separated into two parallel timelines, with video on the top and audio on the bottom.
- **Viewer:** The viewer window shows a preview of the current position in your timeline or a selected shot from the library. The viewer window usually has a play button so you can watch the current clip or sequence.
- **Other features:** Some programs have an *inspector* or *info* window where you can edit properties of the currently selected clip (size, speed, position, and so on). Other programs let you adjust those properties directly from the viewer. Some programs also have *toolbars* where you can choose from various tools for cutting a clip, grabbing a clip, adjusting the audio level, and so on.

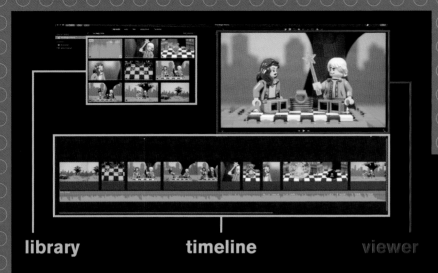

library **timeline** **viewer**

Most editing programs have library, timeline, and viewer windows. Here's what they look like in iMovie. Advanced programs might have additional sections or toolbars.

Step 2: Import Your Footage

After you've finished filming your animation, you'll need to get that footage into your editing software. The particulars of this step will depend on your camera and stop-motion software setup.

If you used stop-motion software, you should be able to export each shot from your stop-motion program and then import those video files into your editing software. Make sure that your frame rate is correct when exporting the video files.

If you shot without stop-motion software, you'll have to download the images from your camera, directly import them into your editing software, and then create your sequence using all the individual images. Another option is to use an image-sequencing program to convert your images into video files and then import those files into your editing software.

Many programs have a dedicated importing interface for adding files to your project library. They might also allow you to drag and drop files directly into your timeline from a file folder on your computer.

> IF YOU'RE FOLLOWING THE PLAN APPROACH, STEPS 3 AND 4 SHOULD BE DONE DURING THE STORYBOARDING AND ANIMATIC PHASES, BEFORE YOU START ANIMATING.

Step 3: Sequence Your Shots

As we discussed in Chapter 7, you might sometimes end up animating the shots of your film out of order. Once you've imported those shots into the editing program, it's time to put them in their final order. If you followed the Plan Approach and created an animatic or a numbered shot list, you can use that as a guide to arranging your shots. If you followed the Play Approach and made up the story as you went along, you'll need to decide how to order the shots. Try rearranging them and then playing them back. Will the audience understand what's happening?

When making *The Magic Picnic*, we filmed shots with similar compositions back-to-back and then rearranged them into story order during the editing process.

FILMING ORDER

| medium shots of minifigs | close-up shots of blanket | wide shots of hillside |

STORY ORDER

Step 4: Trim and Delete Unnecessary Shots

Once you've put the shots into story order, watch your film from beginning to end a few times. As you watch, pay attention to the pacing and flow. Does every shot add something to the story, or could you remove or shorten some shots and still have the story make sense? Maybe that long shot of someone walking down the street only needs to be 5 seconds instead of 8 seconds. It can be painful to cut out animation that you put a lot of time and effort into, but if it's not helping to tell the story, it may confuse or bore your audience.

We don't need to see David's entire walk to the movie theater to understand where he's going; shots 1 and 2 can probably be cut.

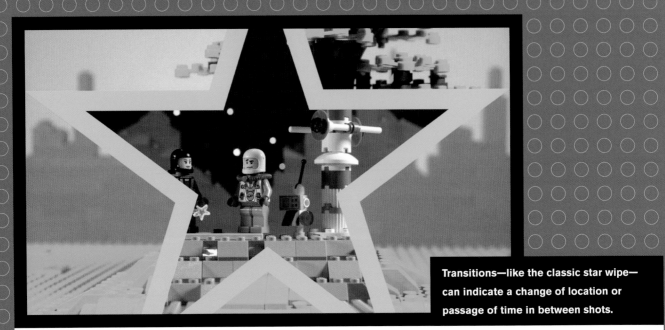

Transitions—like the classic star wipe— can indicate a change of location or passage of time in between shots.

Step 5: Add Transitions

Now that you've got your shots in the right order and trimmed all the excess, you can also spruce things up by adding transitions and visual effects.

A *transition* is a way to connect two shots that helps the audience understand how those shots relate and informs the story you're telling. The default transition is a *cut*: an instant change from one shot to the next. But there are other transition options that, while used less frequently than cuts, can give your audience additional information or set a tone.

- A *dissolve* (also known as a *crossfade*) makes one image fade into another and can indicate a passage of time or a change in location.
- A *fade* is a type of dissolve, usually to a single color. A fade to black is like a visual punctuation mark, signaling the end of a major scene and the beginning of a new one. A fade from black is like a sunrise, alerting the audience that a new day or chapter of the story is beginning. Fading to or from white instead of black can imply an air of calm or a dreamlike state.
- A *wipe* is when one shot is replaced by another through the use of a straight line or shape. Wipes can be used to show the passage of time or a change in location. Some common wipes include horizontal wipes, vertical wipes, clock wipes, and star wipes.
- An *iris in/out* is a particular kind of wipe where one shot enters or exits via an expanding or contracting circle, like a camera shutter snapping a photo. The center of the iris can also draw attention to a specific image or character.

Dissolve

Fade

Wipe

Iris in

Step 6: Add Digital Effects

Next, you can add in digital effects that change the overall look of your shot. For instance, you could flip your shot like a mirror, add a filter to make it black and white, mask out support rigs (see Chapter 2), or draw digital mouths on your characters. When it comes to adding digital effects, the only limits are your imagination, your skill level, and time.

This is also a good time to clean up or adjust the picture. That might mean doing some color correction to make the colors more vibrant or adding some zooming, cropping, or panning to give the appearance of camera movement or to mask a set bump. These effects may be subtle, but they can add a lot of polish to your film. If your camera didn't shoot at the aspect ratio you wanted (see Chapter 8), now is the time to change that.

Digital effects can drastically change the look and feel of a shot.

Original

Flipped

Fisheye

Black and white

Step 7: Add Titles and Credits

Finally, you may want to add an opening title and closing credits to your film. These tell the audience what your film is called and who made it. Most editing programs include a feature for creating simple text titles. You can edit the size, font, and color of the titles right inside the program. You can also add subtitles if you have a character who speaks in a different language than your audience.

Just like every other part of the filmmaking process, creating titles is an opportunity to express your creativity and communicate important information to the audience. The color and font of your titles can help set the tone of the film.

The style of your title card sets the tone for your film—is it serious or lighthearted, simple or fancy?

The Magic Picnic

THE MAGIC PICNIC

THE MAGIC PICNIC

The Magic Picnic

Step 8: Add Music and Sound

Once you've got your video timeline finalized, it's time to turn to the audio timeline. Drag your audio files from the library to the timeline, and position them so that they sync up with what's happening onscreen. For instance, make sure to have the quack sound play just as the duck opens its bill. Try moving the sound forward and backward a couple of frames to see if tweaking the position makes the sound fit better with the video.

Sometimes you'll want to have a sound start before or end after the related action. This is a way to tell the audience about what's happening offscreen. For instance, if you have a shot of one character walking away from another character who is standing still, you might continue the sound of footsteps while the video cuts away from the walker to show the stander's reaction. The noise of the footsteps is still there, because the walker is still within "earshot" of the camera, even though the camera is no longer focused on the walker.

When adding music to your film, you might also want to add audio transitions so that the sound fades in or out to match the action onscreen. If your film has dialogue, make sure that it syncs up with your characters' movements. You can try shortening or extending a visual clip by a few frames to make it match the sound better.

The sound of Matt's footsteps continues to play even after he has left the frame.

IF YOU'RE A PLANNER LIKE ME, ADDING THE DIALOGUE IN LAST PROBABLY FEELS REALLY BACKWARD. THE DIALOGUE TRACK IS USUALLY THE FIRST THING I EDIT. THEN I ANIMATE MY CHARACTERS TO MATCH THE DIALOGUE.

FOR SOME OF MY EARLY FILMS, I WROTE SCRIPTS AFTER ANIMATION AND EDITING WAS COMPLETE. MY VOICE ACTORS AND I WOULD WATCH THE FILM AND IMPROVISE DIALOGUE TO FIT THE ANIMATION.

Advanced Post-production

Post-production can allow you to create some amazing digital effects; however, many of them require a lot of skill and manual labor. The techniques we're about to discuss are not for beginners. If you don't have a lot of experience with post-production software, these might be too complex for you. Once you've built up your skill base doing simple edits, you can try some of these more advanced techniques. Until then, stick to the brick-built effects approach we discussed in Chapter 4.

"Don't worry, Matt, we'll fix it in post-production . . . with MAGIC!"

By layering and resizing clips in a video-editing program, you can combine two shots into one.

Compositing

Compositing is when you animate two or more elements separately and then combine them so they look like one single shot. Ideally, the audience won't be able to tell that you did this. It should look totally natural in the end.

If you are compositing simple rectangular clips together, you can usually accomplish this simply by layering the clips and cropping and resizing them. If you need to composite a moving character onto a totally different background, however, you might need to use a green screen and chroma keying.

When filming against a *green screen*, you don't actually need the screen to be green—it can be any color you want. You just need to make sure the color of your background screen is not used by any other object you're filming in that shot. For instance, if you're filming a green dragon, you might want to use a blue or pink screen instead.

Once you have the clip in your editing software, you can use the chroma key video effect to remove the green screen background color. A *chroma key* takes a specified color and turns it into a transparent area. Then composite the character onto any background you want. The background will show through the transparent area of the chroma-keyed clip.

Step 1: Film your character against a color that will be easy to remove—in this case, blue.

Step 2: Use a chroma key in your editing software to remove the colored background so that the character is now against a transparent background.

Step 3: Film your new background.

Step 4: Composite the character onto the new background.

Lip-Sync Prep Work

If you're planning to do replacement-animation lip sync with your characters (as we discussed in Chapter 2), it's a good idea to do some prep work before animating. You'll want to figure out which mouth shape you'll use in each frame of the animation. You can do this in most animation software by importing the audio clip of the dialogue and the still images of your face shapes. Then you can assign the face shapes to the relevant frames and preview what it will look like. You don't need to assign a unique mouth shape to every single sound; the mouth animation will actually look more natural if certain syllables or sounds are skipped.

When you're ready to animate, the information about which mouth shape to use for each frame will already be in your X-sheet. All you have to do is follow along and put the right mouth on your character at that moment.

Many stop-motion programs allow you to match mouth shapes to audio before you animate.

If you do the lip-sync prep work, then when it's time to animate, you can simply follow the mouth shape guidelines in your X-sheet.

Digital Facial Animation

One of the most complex digital effects in brickfilming is *digital facial animation*—adding facial expressions to a character digitally, frame-by-frame. This technique allows an animator complete control over minifigure facial expressions, but it can require a lot of effort and advanced technical skills.

While the most common use of digital facial animation is to add lip sync, it can also be used to make your minifigs show emotion without saying a word. A great example of this is the film *A Fixed System* by Aaron Fisher.

Follow these steps to create digital facial animations:

1. **Animate your shots with digital effects in mind.** When you're planning to add digital facial animation to a shot, be thoughtful about where the characters' heads are. If they move around a lot, it will be more complicated to add the digital effects. Adding digital faces is easiest when a character looks straight ahead at the camera and their head doesn't move at all. If you're planning to animate every element on your characters' faces, you may want to replace your minifigures' heads with blank heads during filming.

For the opening shot of *The Magic Picnic*, we animated Anna's mouth to match her dialogue. To keep things simple, we filmed her straight on and had her sit still.

2. **Create a set of digital faces or face elements.** Use the image creation software you're most comfortable with (we used Adobe Illustrator) to illustrate the various facial elements you want to animate on your characters. Ideally, these should be vector images on a transparent background. You can download a set of mouth shapes that we created for Anna from the book's website at *https://www.nostarch.com/legoanimation/*.

3. **Composite the facial elements onto the shot.** Depending on your preference, you can either composite facial elements frame-by-frame in an image-editing program or composite them in your video-editing program. One advantage to compositing them in a video-editing program like Adobe After Effects is that you can line up the face elements with your characters' heads without having to redraw them from scratch.

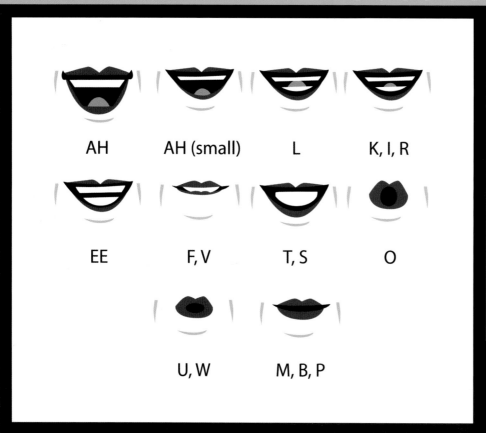

AH   AH (small)   L   K, I, R

EE   F, V   T, S   O

U, W   M, B, P

We wanted to animate only Anna's mouth, so that's the part of her face that we drew digitally.

Sharing Your Film

Once you've got your film looking and sounding great, it's time to share it with the world!

- Export your movie from your editing software as a high-quality video file. You can then use this file to share your film in a variety of formats: DVD, Blu-ray, YouTube, Vimeo, and so on.
- Consider hosting a viewing party at your house and inviting your friends and family. Nothing beats watching your movie in a room full of people. (Don't forget the popcorn!)
- Be on the lookout for festivals and contests to submit your film to. There are even a few brickfilm-specific festivals and contests! We've listed some of them on the book's website (*https://www.nostarch.com/legoanimation/*).

- If you plan to share your film online, consider producing promotional materials like a movie poster, a film trailer, and a short plot synopsis. These can help entice new viewers.
- Share your film with other brickfilmers to get critical feedback (see the book's website for suggested sites and forums).

I LIKE TO SHARE MY FILMS ON VHS! IT'S THE FORMAT OF THE FUTURE.

WITH THE PRESS OF A BUTTON, I CAN NOTIFY THOUSANDS OF PEOPLE AROUND THE WORLD ABOUT MY LATEST MOVIE. I HOPE THEY DON'T NOTICE ALL THE MISTAKES.

Conclusion

So here we are! You've put together your first film—or, at the very least, you've checked another book off of your reading list. You may now be wondering: Where do I go from here? What should I study if I want to turn animation into a career? Do I need to make hundreds of films before I can officially call myself an animator?

As far as we're concerned, you are what you do. If you animate things, you're an animator. If you make films, you're a filmmaker. And anyone who creates art of any kind is a creator, an artist, a maker. This now includes you. Welcome to the club!

Being a creator comes with an obligation to create in a conscientious way. Both Voltaire and Uncle Ben were right: "with great power comes great responsibility." You now have the power to make art that can affect people's minds and lives. Will it make them think? Will it delight and surprise them? Use your powers for good, and make the world a better place.

All animators and filmmakers are creators, as are painters, sculptors, magicians, musicians, beauticians . . .

Giving and Receiving Feedback

As you grow as a creator, you will find yourself giving and receiving critical feedback. This is an important part of the creative process, although it can sometimes be uncomfortable. But giving constructive feedback is a skill like any other, and it gets easier with thoughtful practice.

When giving feedback to others, think about how you might feel if someone said it to you. Remember that it's just as important to share the things you liked ("The voice acting and plot twists were great!") as it is to share the things that didn't work for you ("I noticed there was a lot of light flicker"). The "feedback sandwich" is a good rule of thumb—start and end your feedback with positive comments so that the creator feels supported, not attacked.

We recommend workshopping your films with friends so that you can get feedback on what is and isn't working before your film is complete. When receiving feedback on your work, try not to take it personally. And remember that you don't have to agree with every critique you receive. If the feedback doesn't seem helpful, ignore it and move on. If it is helpful, figure out how to implement it and thank the person who shared it.

Both tomatoes and critical feedback are easier to receive in sandwiches than thrown individually.

What Next?

Throughout this book, we introduced you to many facets of the filmmaking process. Which part did you like the most?

If you enjoyed coming up with stories and writing scripts (Chapter 7), you might want to study creative writing, screenwriting, or something related, like comparative literature. If cinematography (Chapter 8) was more your style, you could study traditional still photography, videography, or general film production. If your favorite part was post-production (Chapter 9), you might focus on video editing, visual effects, or computer graphics. One of the joys of filmmaking is that it uses skills from both the sciences and the humanities—learning math, physics, or anatomy can be just as helpful as studying language, philosophy, or acting.

If you'd like to learn more about LEGO animation specifically, there are a number of online resources. Our favorite online community is Bricks in Motion, and we've listed many additional resources on the book's website (*https://www.nostarch.com/legoanimation/*) so you can explore them yourself. We also maintain a blog called *The Set Bump*, where we highlight noteworthy LEGO animations, brickfilm contests, and other interesting stuff.

You might also be interested in the books *The Illusion of Life: Disney Animation* by Frank Thomas and Ollie Johnston, *The Animator's Survival Kit* by Richard Williams, and *Brick Flicks* by Sarah Herman.

Have Fun!

Telling you to have fun while making movies using a *toy* may seem redundant, but when you're working on a long, involved project, it's possible to get overwhelmed by the work and forget why you started making it in the first place. So it bears repeating: making brickfilms should be fun.

This is true whether you're making a comedic film or a serious one. If you start to feel like you're in a rut or you've stopped enjoying what you're doing, try something different. Change up the story, experiment with new animation techniques, or just take a break and allow your creative batteries to recharge. Your best creative work will come from a place of excitement and possibility, not from a sense of obligation. Or—to put it another way—play well!

WAIT! THE BOOK CAN'T BE OVER! WE DIDN'T GET TO TALK ABOUT DEPTH OF FIELD OR MOTION CONTROL RIGS OR SWIM CYCLES...

GREAT POINT, DAVID! BUT WE ONLY HAVE SO MANY WORDS IN THIS BOOK, AND TH—

Acknowledgments

This book wouldn't have been possible without the contributions of a huge number of people. We would like to thank our editors at No Starch Press for turning our ideas into a book; Valerie Champagne, Erin Natal, and Matt Witham for building, sorting, designing, animating, and so much more; Jennifer and Sam Bourne for photographing us; Joe Meno for publishing our initial articles about LEGO animation in *BrickJournal* issue 14; Larry Beckler and Mike Walter for helping us get officially into business; Marc-André Caron, thefourmonkeys, and Jackson Dame for writing for *The Set Bump*; Bryan and Kathie Bonahoom for organizing Brickworld (where we first met and workshopped a lot of this book); Tormod Askildsen, Kevin Hinkle, and the rest of the Community Team for creating a connection between LEGO fans and The LEGO Group; the brickfilming community for being a constant source of support and inspiration; and all the teachers who let us make videos when we were supposed to be writing papers.

David Pagano: I would like to thank Carol and Lenny for showing me how to think, laugh, rhyme, and improvise and for teaching me the equal importance of art and craft; Mark and Chris for 20+ years of assistance and starring roles; Alex for her entrepreneurial wisdom; Sean Kenney and his team for their support and insight (and for lending us an obscene amount of bricks); John, Dean, Laura, Phil, Rob, Sonya, and all my other professors and classmates for helping me realize that I love both learning and teaching; Kathy, Bruce, and Steven for providing early work opportunities and HQ Legology; Maria and Tony for introducing me to media, culture, and contract negotiations; Aunt Barbara for buying me that first LEGO set; Abokor for being the original audience of Paganomation Home Video; Grandma for supporting me through my various career tangents; the extended Paganomation crew—Jeff, Mick, Nelson, Cynthea, Sarah, Joey, Heidi, Steve, Andrew, Zach, Katie, Kori, Nat, Tom, Ben, and everyone else who's ever lent a hand; my subscribers, backers, followers, and fans; and all of my other friends and family, young and old, here and gone.

David Pickett: I would like to thank Bert for loving and supporting me each and every day through crises large and small; Jack and Linda for encouraging me in countless ways since the day I was born; Jenny and JP for shaping my creativity and sense of humor; Adam and Jeremy for being my first animation collaborators and donating their LEGO collections to me; Eleanor for always helping me weed out my least practical ideas; Cin for teaching me the power of my voice; Achy for teaching me how to workshop a book; Kitty for teaching me that language is more than just words; Fire Escape Films for providing me with a network of friends and collaborators; and my YouTube audience for giving me the financial freedom to live my dream.

Index

V

vertical (y-axis) shot movement, 161
very wide shot (VWS), 158
video recording (camera), 113
viewer window (editing software), 180
VWS (very wide shot), 158

W

waist (minifigure articulation), 17
walk cycle, 25–26
walking, 24–27, 55
webcams, 116
weight, adding to animation, 45, 46–47
"what if?" question, 141
white balance, 129, 173
wide shot (WS), 158
Williams, Richard, 199
wipe transition, 184, 185
wrists (minifigure articulation), 16
WS (wide shot), 158

X

x-axis (horizontal) shot movement, 160
X-sheets (exposure sheets), 132, 151–152

Y

y-axis (vertical) shot movement, 161

Z

z-axis (depth) shot movement, 162
zooming, 162